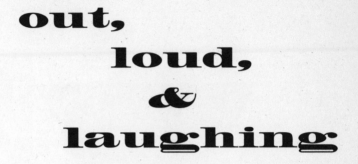

out, loud, & laughing

A Collection of Gay & Lesbian Humor

Edited by
Charles Flowers

Anchor Books
Doubleday
New York London
Toronto Sydney Auckland

AN ANCHOR BOOK
PUBLISHED BY DOUBLEDAY
a division of Bantam Doubleday Dell Publishing Group, Inc.
1540 Broadway, New York, New York 10036

ANCHOR BOOKS, DOUBLEDAY, and the portrayal of an
anchor are trademarks of Doubleday, a division of Bantam
Doubleday Dell Publishing Group, Inc.

This anthology is a work of humor. Any references to real
people are used only to convey the contributors' satirical
purposes and are not to be taken literally.

Acknowledgments for individual works appear on pages 203–
206.

Book design by F.J. Levine

Library of Congress Cataloging-in-Publication Data

Out, loud, & laughing : a collection of gay and lesbian humor
/ edited by Charles Flowers.
     p.   cm.
   1. Homosexuality—Humor.   I. Flowers, Charles,
1965– .
  II. Title: Out, loud, and laughing.
  PN6231.H57098   1995
  817'.54080353—dc20   94-32709
                                         CIP

ISBN 0-385-47618-3

contents

editor's note

The idea for a collection of gay and lesbian humor first came to me in late 1993, a year in which openly gay and lesbian comics appeared everywhere: bookstores, comedy clubs, off-Broadway, university campuses, *The Arsenio Hall Show, The Joan Rivers Show, Roseanne,* even CNN (thanks to the 1993 March on Washington). Suddenly, America was laughing *with* gays and lesbians, rather than *at* them. This flurry of visibility hit a significant peak in December 1993, when Comedy Central aired its first all-gay and -lesbian comedy special, *Out There,* which received the channel's highest-ever ratings and generated a sequel, *Out There II,* which aired in October 1994.

I knew the project had commercial potential, but I began to consider the book's purpose more closely when the Publishing Triangle, a New York–based professional organization for gays and lesbians in publishing, held a panel discussion entitled "Out Lesbian and Gay Humor: On the Page, On the Stage, and In the Comedy Clubs." Moderated by Frank DeCaro of

New York Newsday, the panel assembled a variety of performers and writers to discuss what constitutes "out" gay and lesbian humor. The program teased the audience by listing questions like "Are lesbians funny?" "Do lesbians know that lesbians are funny?" For over two hours humor was taken seriously as panelists tossed about some larger questions—"Can a straight audience appreciate a gay joke?" "How PC does one have to be?" —before agreeing that the increased presence of openly gay and lesbian humorists could only be a good thing and that each individual comic should strive to be as funny as possible.

What struck me most was that the discussion echoed many debates of inclusion/exclusion heard across America today. The particular focus was humor, but the same issues of definition and legitimacy appear in other arenas where gay and lesbian Americans are making their presence known. Gays in the military. Lesbian parents. Gay and lesbian couples getting married. Everywhere you turn, we are in the news—and more often than not, at the center of some controversy, some debate about tolerance and civil rights, where anger and hatred rule the day. Some of these conflicts stem, I believe, from America's inability to accept a central contradiction: gay and lesbian people are the same as everybody else AND gay and lesbian people are different from everybody else. Americans like to keep things simple —white or black, male or female, straight or gay—and so we tend to live our lives in absolute terms: if you're different from me, then you're *completely* different from me. Same or different —no middle ground. I like to think, however, that we possess a common humanity, which is shaped, but not erased by, differences like sexual orientation. At our core, gays and lesbians are the same as other Americans, yet our sexual orientation does create cultural differences, which, in turn, are affected by our other differences, like gender or class.

What does this have to do with humor? Like our ability to reason, our capacity to laugh and to make one another laugh seems a genuinely universal human trait and one we've developed to an art form. Humor can be as easy as a pratfall or as complicated as satire, yet the effect is singular: a moment of release when laughter takes hold. That moment of vulnerability is crucial because it enables humor to be truly progressive, in the sense of creating change, both personal and collective. Think about it. People make jokes about what they fear. Airplanes. Doctors. Dating. Parenting. The more anxiety there is around a subject, the greater potential for laughter, which cuts away at that anxiety. Another contradiction to accept. In that giggle or chuckle or belly laugh, we drop our defenses and identify with the comedian, who assures us we are not alone. In a sense, we join a community when we laugh and forget the differences—real and imagined—which separate us. What remains after the laughter is the sense of pleasure, of identification rather than difference, which lets us remember our common bond. If the comedian is gay or black or feminist, that identification just might create cultural change by connecting us with a person we might otherwise consider alien or threatening.

In editing this anthology, I looked for humor which spoke to both the differences and the similarities of gay and lesbian people with the rest of America. How this translates is that we have gay and lesbian comic riffs on dating etiquette, home shopping, the younger generation, talk shows, sex, cats (of course), the possibly lethal repercussions of Lesbian Chic, growing up in the suburbs, living in the big cities, the "Q" word, body piercing, unrequited love for k.d. lang (even the men), uniform fetishes, control queens, dreading gym class but loving the gym, forgiving parents, commitment (really!), *Jeopardy!*, growing old, and terrorizing Pat Buchanan, Jesse Helms, and Pat Robertson.

Ironically, a lot of these pieces find their sources in childhood and adolescence, a time when gays and lesbians seem to suffer the most, when hearing a faggot joke in the schoolyard or a whisper of "dyke" in the bathroom affects a child's sense of self for years to come. As adults, these contributors are certainly having the last laugh, and they take aim as well at stereotypes we have all endured: the limp wrists and flannel shirts, decorator tastes and truck-driving skills. Some of these pieces reject such cultural images of gays and lesbians outright, while others refashion them on their own terms. There is a freedom in this sort of humor, an ability to self-parody, not with shame but with laughter, which makes this anthology fiercely proud and reveals a strength I first witnessed, surprisingly, on TV. It was Billy Crystal, as Jodie on the late 1970s sitcom *Soap*, who told the first gay-positive joke I ever heard: When questioned if he was a practicing homosexual, Jodie calmly replied, "No, I'm not. I don't have to practice; I'm good at it." That one-liner enabled me—a closeted adolescent—to see humor in being gay, and I soon realized how humor provided a way of dealing with the world, its harsh homophobia, and my fear of being gay. As a community, gays and lesbians have long supported and worshiped their comedians, the people who make us laugh and somehow render our lives less stigmatized and more human.

In a July 1993 poll on what straight America thinks of gay

America, *U.S. News & World Report* reported that "53% of American voters say they personally know someone who is gay and this familiarity tends to make them think more favorably about gay rights," while the other 46% said "they do not know anyone gay and they largely oppose gay rights." If knowing someone gay can make a crucial difference in the gay and lesbian struggle for acceptance, how do we get to know that someone? I can think of no better way than by listening to them explain their childhood or rant about the government or complain about dieting or laugh at their own queer habits. This anthology's primary purpose is to entertain, but in a larger sense, these contributors are introducing gay and lesbian Americans to the rest of America. Their out, loud, and definitely proud voices celebrate being gay, being human, and being able to laugh. In the words of W. E. B. Du Bois, laughter is "a divine gift [which] has made the world human and lovable, despite all its pain and wrongs." Gay and lesbian humor is such a gift, to be valued and to be shared, and in the laughter it gives to America, this collection aspires to serve humor's greater purpose.

Charles Flowers
August 1994
New York City

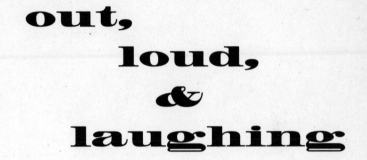

out,
loud,
&
laughing

kate clinton is a nationally known humorist and writer.

kate clinton

Could Lesbians Return?

(written when the *Newsweek* "Lesbians" cover story appeared the week after the "Could Dinosaurs Return?" cover story)

NEWS BULLETIN, the year 8093—Paleoarcheologists have discovered an ancient mosquito suspended in amber resin in a dig outside a known lesbian festival site in northern Michigan. Scientists were studying the foundation of an ancient "eatery," complete with ceremonial food arches, when they chanced upon the find. The excellent condition of the site also enabled them to uncover a small container of carbon foodsticks labeled "Dino-Fries."

Hypothesizing that the lambent mosquito had bitten a lesbian attending the festival, scientists used a syringe found in a diet Pepsi can to extract blood from the mosquito's perfectly preserved and engorged proboscis and isolated an incomplete strand of DNA. They augmented the partial strand of DNA with the DNA from a leather softball cover, circa 1991, and using ordinary tap water, rehydrated the complete DNA and *ecce lesbo*! A reanimated lesbian.

"This is an extraordinary moment," said project spokesperson Simone Noway, "for it has allowed us to end our centuries-long speculation about what caused the lesbian to become extinct. As soon as 'Amber' came around, we were able to talk to her and find out what happened in those crucial latter years of the twenty-first century."

Archeologists at Hetrick-Martin University had led research in the field for years, pioneering dig techniques at sites all over North America and proffering several intriguing theories on lesbian extinction.

In 7969, "Stonewall Six Thousand," at an East Coast urban site, they uncovered scuffed, but perfectly intact Vibram-soled footwear, "Doc Martens," which still had a half life of about a billion years. Scientists speculated that their huge, weighted soles made it difficult for lesbians to flee from their predators. "We believe that in some cases, especially in the larger-sized footwear, lesbians undecided on this style looked down at their feet and actually died of fright. The later platform style was apparently quite lethal," said Noway.

In 7890, Western water workers chanced upon the site of the second Lesbian Herstory Archives. The treasure trove yielded up invaluable information from the late 1900s, a crucial period in lesbian evolution. Artifacts found at that site refuted the earlier-held notion that some drastic environmental or climatic change, some hole in the ozone layer ("bigger than Perry Watkins's nose ring"—unclear cultural referent, but very funny to many at the time), caused the Great Dyke Demise.

After poring over archival information, scientists speculated that in fact the sudden glare of media publicity was too much for the lesbian organism. "After living mushroomlike for years in the primordial ooze of rumor and innuendo, lesbians were sent into shock by the 'Lesbian Chic Period,' following as it did so hard on the heels of the 'Stealth Lesbian Era.' Despite an emergency airlift of cool sunglasses from L.A. Eyeworks, many perished from squinting."

Perhaps the most controversial theory was presented at the 6100th Annual Women's Studies Conference by Professor Mookie McClinton, famous for her ovual work, *Lesbian Family Trees: The Burning Bush*. In her thesis on the dyke diaspora, "Lesbo a Go-Go?" she stated, "I believe, quite simply, that they ate their own. And I don't mean that in the good, old way," she added wryly. "It's no coincidence that at that same time, the mainstream, swollen from assimilating many tributaries, overflowed its banks. Not only were food sources destroyed, but weak dykes were blamed. It was *The Hunger* part two redux *pas de deux* all over."

Scientists briefed a slightly dazed Amber, wearing multipocketed pants and a NO ONE KNOWS I'M A LESBIAN T-shirt, very popular in the Irony Age of the late 1900s. She rejected the shoe, sunlight, and snack theories. "NOA," she said flatly.

"None of the above. Here's what happened. Cruises became popular. Especially after the pictures of gay sailors. RSVP Cruises started doing submarine cruises. And the Aqua-Separatists sailed everywhere: Alaska—"The Klondikes"; Australia —"The Down There Trip;" Lesbos—"The Redundancy Tour." Not me. I believe a navy of ex-lovers cannot sail. I was actually one of the last land-based lesbians.

"Anyway, they ran out of places to go. At the time of my tragic accident, a mud-wrestling top-bottom thing, I know plans were in the works for a huge cruise to Jupiter. They'd be gone seven thousand years, stop at other planets out and back, with a different show every night. There were just that many lesbian comedians then. Lesbian liftoff was scheduled for late 1993. Near as I can figure, they'll be back soon, give or take a month."

jaffe cohen is best known as one of the first openly gay comedians to appear on network television. In addition to his initial appearance on FOX–TV's *Comic Strip Live,* he has also appeared on *The Joan Rivers Show* and CNBC's *Real Personal.* Since 1989 he's been criss-crossing the country with Bob Smith and Danny McWilliams as Funny Gay Males, the award-winning trio of comics who broke new ground when they appeared at the prestigious Just for Laughs Festival in Montreal. In 1993 the group performed at Alan King's Toyota Comedy Festival as well as during the March on Washington.

Cohen is also an accomplished writer, his comic essays and interviews having appeared in *Outweek, New York Native, QW, 10 Percent,* and *The Harvard Gay and Lesbian Review.* Cohen collaborated with FGM on *Growing Up Gay,* which will be published by Hyperion in the spring of 1995. Earlier works include the plays *Elliot of Arabia* and *Elliot Bound;* an independent film, *Chicken of the Sea;* and a comedy revue, *Gay Gezundt.* In the spring of 1994 his one-man play, *My Life as a Christian,* ran for eight weeks at the historic Courtyard Playhouse in Greenwich Village. Currently he's writing a novel. So far he just has the title: *Portrait of a Narcissist as a Young Man.*

jaffe cohen

My Life as a Heterosexual

My parents have always loved me, but they've never been able to give me exactly what I wanted. If I asked for watermelon, my mother bought me cantaloupe; if I wanted to borrow the car, my father would offer to drive me. It's not that I wasn't a star in the household—but being a star meant that I was off in outer space—light years away in relation to them—so that by the time either one of them became minutely aware of what I wanted, the desire had often burned out and they were only responding to the afterglow. Lately I've been thinking that most parents can't really grow with their children—but perhaps this is for the best. This is nature's way of telling us that we have to leave our parents in order to find fulfillment. I know this because I might still be living in the suburbs if twenty years ago my parents had been just a little more understanding.

At that time I was living in a development on Long Island. A development, if you can picture it, is a cross between a potato farm and an actual neighborhood. After World War II, developers ripped out the spuds and replaced them with identical houses built out of the same cardboard as my loose-leaf note-book. These tract houses were attractive to couples with young kids because the roads were built crooked in such a way that cars crawled through them, and children were allowed to play safely in the middle of the streets; that's all you ever saw in developments, children playing in the middle of empty streets. There were no stores, no businesses, no minorities. In short, developments were ideal environments for growing up totally ignorant and bored.

In 1969 I was still living with my parents, not an unusual choice for a fifteen-year-old, and I was just starting to figure out that my passion for persons of my own sex was not some-thing I would outgrow anytime soon. What was even more worrisome was that I had no passion for the opposite sex. I had been able to disguise this fact by nodding agreeably at appropri-ate moments when the other guys talked about girls; but I had now reached an age when the girls themselves would expect me to put out. I was worried.

Then one Saturday morning, the summer before my senior year in high school, I came downstairs and found the house empty. There was a newspaper sitting on the dining room ta-ble, and on the cover was a picture of a man in a woman's dress (I didn't yet know the proper title of "drag queen") and this "homosexual activist" was being shoved kicking and screaming into the back of a police van. My first thought was "At least I'm not that fucked up," and my second thought was "I better hide this paper before anyone thinks I am." So I threw the paper into the back of the closet with all the other periodicals being readied for the trash. I might just as well have crawled in there myself because that was the day I resolved to live at least one more year as a heterosexual.

So my senior year in high school I had two girlfriends, the first of whom was Rosalie DiPasquale, a sleek Italian girl with long brown hair that reached the small of her back. She smelled good and had pretty teeth and I was proud to walk her down the hall. We met in the backseat of a car; we had driver's ed the same period. My helplessness behind the wheel appealed to her because, as I later found out, Rosalie, although very attractive, fancied herself frigid. Her previous boyfriend, Vito, was arrogant and had failed to arouse her sexually. One might say that after being mauled by a real man, she was now ready for something completely different.

One day in late September, while watching me struggle to parallel park, she got the idea that I was the guy for her. Later that week I walked her home and we sat together on a rusty swing set in her parents' backyard. She confessed to me that her biggest fear was that she would never find someone she could trust; and, at the age of sixteen, she was certain that she'd live and die a virgin. On the other hand, she did feel safe and warm around me. Could I possibly be the one who would save her from a life devoid of passion?

I had no idea what to say, so I kissed her, trying my best to remember how it was done in the movies. I tilted my head back so my glasses wouldn't poke out her eye. After a few moments Rosalie leaned away from me and monitored her biological responses. Her face was flushed. My clumsiness had moved something deep inside of her. Then she kissed me again, and for the next six months the two of us were inseparable.

We were an odd couple, a Jewish geek and an Italian cheer-leader, but 1969 was also the year of Woodstock and Rosalie was starting to break free of the development herself. At first she reveled in the oddness of our association. She enjoyed flaunting me in front of her cheerleader friends, and more than that, she enjoyed annoying her strict Italian father, who, until recently, had ruled his house like Mussolini. So it was only a matter of time before Rosalie's dad got tired of coming home from work and finding me sitting in his favorite recliner and eating his Fritos. He badgered Rosalie constantly about my presence, and sometime in February he convinced his daughter to give me up for Lent.

Rosalie was miserable when she told me this, but I was secretly relieved. For a time going out with Rosalie had been ideal because I was so worried about her frigidity that I almost forgot that I was gay. Sometime in November, however, Rosa-lie's younger brother Danny had started developing secondary sexual characteristics, and by February he was much more at-tractive to me than his sister. With a young hunk like that in the house, I would need to go somewhere else if I wanted to be heterosexual; and—as long as I was being traditional—I might as well find a girl from my own background, someone who might conceivably bear me Jewish children.

So I started dating Bonnie Garfinkel, whom I'd met at the Young Women's Hebrew Association's Purim Festival. She'd been performing onstage in a reenactment of the ancient bibli-cal tale of Esther, in which she played the second lead, Queen Esther's wisecracking, gum-chewing lady-in-waiting. She was brilliant, funny-looking, and insecure. In fact, she reminded me a lot of myself. I asked her out that very night.

In April Bonnie took me home to meet her family and we ate in the breakfast nook, which was the only area in their house not roped off or covered with plastic. I soon learned that Elaine Garfinkel, Bonnie's mother, only allowed real company to sit in the living room. Elaine also revealed to me that she and her daughter had recently returned from having their noses fixed in Bermuda. The surgeon had given them a family-rate discount, and Bonnie joked that he'd even spayed their poodle as part of the deal.

I was intrigued by Bonnie's family. They lived in a fancy development on the right side of the tracks. Whereas my family was middle-class, at best, Bonnie was the only child of a podiatrist with enough disposable income to replicate, within his home on Long Island, a slightly scaled-down version of the Palace of Versailles. They lived the life to which I should have been aspiring. Rosalie's father had objected to me on religious grounds; Dr. Garfinkel's objections were purely economic. He took one look at me and seriously questioned my ability to earn a living. He asked me what I would ever do in the real world, and I answered with the first thought that came into my head: I'd be a psychiatrist. When the doctor informed me that in order to be a psychiatrist I'd need about twenty-five years of med school, I lowered my voice and replied that I'd not thought that far ahead. Which was the truth. From what I'd seen of the real world I had absolutely no idea what I would do in it.

Meanwhile, Bonnie and I were meeting almost every day to make out in her converted basement on a black leatherette sofa beneath the portrait of a matador. After two hours my lips couldn't have been more numb if I'd been gargling with novocaine. At this point I'd like to make one point perfectly clear about my life as a heterosexual. It wasn't as though Bonnie and Rosalie didn't arouse me physically. It was just that when we were making out together I would get this strange sensation. It was as if I were dispassionately watching myself go through the motions of arousal—not unlike the way my parents saw me—as if from a great, great distance. My heart beat fast and I was as hard as the Wailing Wall, but my soul just wasn't involved. Whenever I left Bonnie's house I felt wistful and sad, as though my real life were being lived elsewhere—in some secret four-dimensional world—only I wasn't there yet to enjoy it.

In June I finally graduated high school and I had to make some decisions about college. What I really wanted to do was stay in my parents' house and go to a community college, but unfortunately I'd graduated fifth in my class and so not going away to a good school would have been like avoiding the draft during World War II. I was paralyzed. I'd sent away for brochures but didn't open my mail when they arrived. Meanwhile, my parents' house was feeling smaller and smaller. Like some retarded chick, I'd outgrown my shell but I hadn't the heart to peck away at the boundaries of my life. Then, like most teenagers, I began avoiding my parents for no reason at all, rushing from the table after dinner to do absolutely nothing. If my mom and dad had asked me why I wasn't more excited about going away to school, I probably would have mumbled something about not wanting to leave Bonnie behind.

What could I have been thinking? Did I really imagine that I'd go on seeing Bonnie for a few more years, go to med school, get married, settle down with a wife and a gaggle of morose, overly complicated children? I must have. I saw no other alternative to the real world of my parents and the Garfinkels. I'd simply have to go on living as a heterosexual, continue being unhappy and, for all intents and purposes, alone.

Then one Saturday in late August, on a whim, I took Bonnie to see the movie *The Boys in the Band*. This was a revelation. The drag queens photographed at the Stonewall Riot had been alien creatures, but these middle-class complainers were people I could relate to. They lived in nice apartments and wore expensive sweaters. I wasn't exactly inspired, but I was confirmed. So what if these guys were miserable; at least they lived in a world to which I could honestly aspire. If only there'd been a hole in the movie screen, I gladly would have crawled through. This movie felt like real life; the acting began after the house lights came up in the theater.

Bonnie was looking at me suspiciously. For two hours I'd been totally unaware of her presence; but there she was, a podiatrist's daughter, looking at me out of the corner of her eye and waiting for me to start making jokes about the movie we'd just seen. We talked about the weather instead. We both agreed that it was getting cooler and that the summer was definitely over.

The next day I woke up severely depressed. I now had a goal for my future, but how would I get there? Looking back, I might have done what millions of other red-blooded American boys had done before me. I could have bought a ticket on the Long Island Railroad, gotten out at Penn Station, and then taken the subway downtown to Christopher Street. But I was hardly the type to travel alone. Nor was I the type to do anything without telling my parents . . .

My parents? If I were ever to become one of those boys in

the band, would my parents then disappear from my life? I loved them as fiercely as they loved me. In a few short days I'd be packed off to a dormitory in another part of the state and I needed to clear the air before leaving home. I needed advice.

Luckily, my mother at this time was seeing a psychiatrist in Jamaica, Queens—a Dr. Dubinsky—and I decided that he was the man I needed to talk to. It was Sunday; classes would begin a week later, the following Monday. I needed to talk to him that very same week. Now, I never could have done this behind my parents' backs—I couldn't afford it—and lest my parents thought that my psychological problem was something really serious, I decided to tell them that I believed myself to be gay.

Whenever I tell people that I came out to my parents at seventeen, I'm usually applauded for my courage. The truth is that I was taking the path of least resistance. I was absolutely miserable; I needed their help in order to see a therapist; and on the night in question my parents hadn't gone bowling. No sooner had I decided to talk to Mom and Dad than their Sunday night league was mysteriously canceled. I wandered downstairs planning a few hours of doing nothing, only to find my mother and father sitting on either end of the couch watching the movie *Spartacus* on the last thirty-inch black-and-white TV set in existence. I sat down between them and pretended to be interested in the flick. Every few minutes my mother would declare, "Oy. That Kirk Douglas. What a handsome man!" And I would squirm in my seat. Could she possibly have already guessed the news I was about to tell her? I resolved to make my announcement during the first commercial break.

The first commercial came and went. I got as far as clearing my throat. Meanwhile, Kirk Douglas was beating back the entire forces of imperial Rome. A heroic gesture was called for. A beer commercial flashed on the screen. My parents didn't care for beer, so I jumped up and turned off the TV set. My father, assuming that I was about to leave the room, yelled at me: "Hey, mister. You're not the only one watching television."

"Oh . . . I'm sorry." I flicked on the set and returned to my seat.

"Ruth," my father said, "he's *your* son."

So I watched the whole movie with them and was almost able to forget my problem. Meanwhile, Kirk Douglas wound up losing the war and being crucified for all his troubles. Then the movie ended and the eleven o'clock news was next. I would gladly have waited for the sports report (my parents don't care for sports either), but my mother stretched her arms and announced, "Well, that's it for me." It was now or never. Beating my mom to her feet, I jumped up, flicked off the set, cleared my throat, and faced my parents head-on. Before there was any time for them to react, I announced, "Mom, Dad. I think I'm . . . I mean, I think I have . . . homosexual feelings and I'd like to talk about them."

My parents were silent.

"Not with you. With a professional . . . so . . ."

My parents nodded their heads and leaned in closer. Apparently I hadn't completed my last sentence. I tried to gauge my parents' reaction thus far. Were they angry? Sad? Relieved that I wasn't telling them something worse? Maybe they were merely waiting for more information. Apparently I hadn't yet said anything that required either one of them to respond.

". . . so . . . I'd like to talk to Dr. Dubinsky." Something in the air began to shift. I continued, "And so I'd like to borrow the car."

My father took a deep breath. At last I was on familiar ground. He turned toward my mother, who kept her eyes on me even as she answered my father's questions.

"Ruth, can Jaffe take your car to Dubinsky's?"

"I think so . . . I . . . What day did you want to go?"

I said the first day that came into my mind: "Tuesday."

"I'm volunteering at the library Tuesday until three. Myron, could you get Jerry Silverman to drive you to work Tuesday morning?"

"That shouldn't be a problem."

"You can take your father's car. Is that all right?"

The three of us nodded our heads in agreement. The first hurdle had been achieved. We sat quietly for another moment before my father pointed his finger at me and asked, "By the way, you know how to get to Dubinsky's?"

"I . . . can probably find it."

"Take the Expressway to Utopia Parkway. That's two exits after the Throgs Neck Bridge. There's the bridge exit, Kissena Boulevard. Then there's Utopia Parkway. What number exit is that, Ruth?"

My mother was shaking her head. "Forget about the Expressway. Take Northern State Parkway. It's faster."

"Only at rush hour. What time were you planning on going?"

"I don't know."

"So let's say he leaves at noon, Ruth. It's still faster to take the Expressway."

"Take the Parkway."

"All right. All right. Listen to your mother. Forget about the Expressway. Take the Parkway and get off at 168th Street."

"188th Street."

"168th."

"188th is faster. Believe me, I go there every week."

"And every week you go the wrong way."

"Myron, I'm sorry, you don't know what you're talking about."

"Do you want me to show you on a map?"

"Myron, don't be ridiculous."

"Take my word on this, son. Don't get off the Parkway until you get to 188th Street in Jamaica."

"All right."

"Ruth, am I right?"

My mother shrugged her shoulders in a way which only conceded that she was too tired to fight. My father was infuriated: "I'll go get the map!" My father stood up and was halfway up the stairs.

"Myron, don't bother!"

"The one thing I know how to do is drive! Would you give me that much?"

"Fine."

When my father left the room, the static died down and the picture came into focus. A mother and a son. I sat there in silence while my mother shifted the weight of her face from two hands to one. Was there anything more that had to be said? Finally, she spoke without looking at me: "Just make sure you get gas before you leave."

"OK."

"The gauge in Dad's car is broken. When it says you have a quarter tank, you really have less."

"Thanks." I stood up, relieved to discover that I still had legs. "I'll see you tomorrow."

"Sleep well, darling."

Then I kissed my mother on the cheek and bounded up the stairs to my room. Shutting the door firmly behind me, I flopped onto my bed and stared at the space between me and the ceiling. Downstairs my father had returned with the map. I heard my parents' voices but was strangely uninterested in what they were saying to each other. I was mainly conscious of the pounding in my chest. I had done it! I had really done it! I'd opened my mouth and said the words. My parents' reaction had been somewhat bizarre, although not completely out of character. Once again they hadn't given me *exactly* what I'd wanted, but that was perfectly all right. I was free. I'd done what I had to do.

I yanked off one of my sneakers and tossed it casually across the room. "What do they know about being gay?" I asked myself. "Nothing." I pulled off my other sneaker and threw it at the first. Then again, what did I know? Not much more. I'd lusted after Rosalie's brother and seen pictures of busted drag queens, but I still had no clear image—I hoped that it would be more fabulous than what had gone before—but I really wasn't sure yet how my life as a homosexual would differ from my life thus far. I just knew that my life as a heterosexual was finally over. I would never again be a confused child playing in empty streets. And I also knew that this phase of my life had ended— not in melodramatics or heavy analysis, but in a discussion of traffic flow patterns and a broken fuel gauge. These symbols of my parents' life—after all—meant nothing to me.

"So, maybe I won't even bother to see the shrink." I took off the rest of my clothes, turned off the lights, and slid under the covers. I lay there in bed with my eyes open and gradually noticed how clearly one could actually see in the dark. Then I imagined myself leaving home the following week and, for the first time all year, started to feel more excited than scared.

sara cytron (comic) and **harriet malinowitz** (chief writer) have been collaborating on a lesbian, feminist stand-up comedy act for the last eight years. *Sojourner* says of them, "It's another Jane Wagner/Lily Tomlin combination —but the *out* version!" Other collaborations include a play, *Minus One,* which Harriet wrote and Sara directed in New York in 1989. Sara has performed their comedy shows *A Dyke Grows in Brooklyn* and *Take My Domestic Partner—Please!* around the country and on television, and has hosted PBS's *In the Life* as Lambda, the Good Butch of the Northeast.

sara cytron

harriet malinowitz

From *A Dyke Grows in Brooklyn* and *Take My Domestic Partner— Please!*

I had a dream that I was the first lesbian President of the United States. They called me President Butch. And Harriet was the First Lover. She not only wanted to redecorate the White House, she wanted to put a nipple on the dome of the Capitol building. At the inauguration Harriet wore a pillbox hat and hiking boots. We appointed an all-lesbian cabinet, and these women were so thrilled not only that they had influential, high-powered, internationally recognized jobs, but also that for the first time in their lives they were guaranteed four years of health insurance. I bulldozed the Pentagon and had it reconstructed as a Pink Triangle—which housed a national artificial insemination center. I abolished the National Guard, and when local disturbances needed quelling, I called in ACT UP. Yes—if there was a school board that refused to hand out condoms, or an outbreak of homophobia on some campus, I, as your commander-in-chief, would call in ACT UP and they'd come tearing in, mounted on horses, yelling "Shame! Shame! Shame!" and the whole situation would be completely resolved.

▼

In 1992 it seemed that we finally had elected a President who cared about our rights. When I think of that election night, I remember feeling like I had been nauseous for twelve years and finally just threw up. I'll admit it: the terror of four more years of right-wing, Republican government made me—a queer, feminist, left-wing radical—actually feel thrilled that we were electing a self-proclaimed moderate centrist who was two-faced and who, in his first seven months, would manage to achieve the popularity rating of Joey Buttafuoco.

But no matter how disappointing he may be in many ways, there is one thing you've got to say about Bill Clinton: the man's into process. He's so into process that sometimes I think Bill Clinton's a lesbian.

And you know he's a Democrat because of Chelsea's hair. No Republican would let their kid have hair like that.

There's actually a gender gap in our community when it comes to Hillary Clinton. Lesbians love her, but gay men still haven't recovered from that outfit she wore on Inauguration Day.

Remember when the Clintons first came in—overturning the gag rule on abortion, funding fetal-tissue research? After such an auspicious beginning, how did he turn out to be such an asshole about the whole issue of lifting the ban against lesbians and gays in the military? Amid this whole uproar, the most apt comment I heard was on my local eleven o'clock TV news when they interviewed a woman on the street. She said, "I don't understand somethin'. These guys are supposed to travel all over the world, live in trenches, sleep in mud, and walk over minefields. But they can't take some guy lookin' at 'em?"

Actually, she's not the only one who's confused. Sometimes, these days, I'm almost as confused by the queer movement as I am by Clinton. I mean, my whole life I've been writing letters to Congress saying the military was an infantilizing, fascist, morally bankrupt force that rapes and kills. And now we're fighting for our right to be a part of it.

But have you noticed that in this whole national debate about lesbians and gays in the military, the media's attention is riveted on men? The big unasked question is what is it going to be like when all those lesbians who have been in the military since the Wacs and the Waves can finally just come out? Forget about "Don't ask, don't tell, don't pursue." We're not going to accept that. There's going to come a time when women entering the military are going to have a big, brazen, butch, no-holds-barred dyke troop commander just waiting to whip them into shape. And this is what she'll have her unit sing as she leads them through a drill in basic training:

> Dolly Parton has big breasts,
> Men have balls, I'm not impressed!

> Over hill and over dale,
> Over Jill and under Gail!

> From the halls of Montezuma,
> They should've let dykes in this battalion sooner!

> *To the shores of Tripoli,*
> *Hey, Sam Nunn, don't mess with me!*

> *Here, Dan Rather, get this scoop:*
> *We're one happy pussy troop!*

That will definitely put hair on their nipples!

Did you go to the March on Washington? I know you didn't! The National Park Service was counting, and they said you weren't there. Not you, not any of your friends, no one from your city, not me. Nobody was there! Three hundred thousand —yeah, sure. Then there's the other statistic that came out at the same time—that one percent of the population is gay. You know, it's true what they say: declining SAT math scores do affect all of us.

I go to a lot of demonstrations in Washington, but I have to confess that I'm just doing my duty. I don't have the same zest for them that a lot of people I know do. Every time I hear that there's going to be a big, national mobilization, I think, "Oh God, no! Not another one!" You know, where you have to shuffle along for three hours till you're totally depleted and exhausted, only there hasn't been a single benefit to your heart, your lungs, or your muscle tone. I call it a Schlep on Washington.

The most horrible thing is that you have to chant. I'm always afraid somebody's going to look at me and catch me not chanting. Then, if I do succumb to peer pressure, I can't believe what it is I have to say. All these chants start with "Hey, hey! Ho, ho!" What are we trying to do—convince the Congress that Santa Claus wants a lesbian and gay civil rights bill?

Then I always feel pressured to raise my fist. Everybody around me is shouting, "What do we want?" I'm thinking, "To put my fist down."

Meanwhile, you're trying to defer the disgusting experience of using the Porta-Johns. When you finally just have to at the end of the day, you're sorry you waited until half a million people went before you.

But this March on Washington was different than any other. The media coverage alone was unprecedented. For several days before the March, you'd turn on *Good Morning America*—there were queers. *Today* show—queers. *Nightline*—queers. *New York Times, Washington Post, Boston Globe*—queers, queers, queers. *USA Today* had a special weekend edition with a pink triangle right in the middle of it. C-SPAN covered the rally live for seven hours. That Monday, social studies teachers had to come up with incredible new questions for their students' current events quizzes. Like, number one: Who is Urvashi Vaid? Number two: Name five states with sodomy laws. (For five extra bonus points, define sodomy.) Number three (short essay question): Imagine that RuPaul decided to enlist in the military. What kinds of obstacles might he face?

This really isn't as far-fetched as it seems. Because one of the main themes of the day was how mainstream we are. I've been to a lot of Marches on Washington, but this was the first time that I was surrounded by people waving American flags, talking about how passionately we want to serve our country, with military planes flying on the video screen and officers and cadets stomping around onstage to military music. We've become so identified with patriotism that I heard Toys "Я" Us is planning to market a GI Martina doll.

It's really true now that *we are everywhere!* We're in the Army, we're in the White House, we're in tennis, we're in the PTA, we're Mom's apple pie. I even saw a leather-dyke mom hanging out near the National Air and Space Museum whose nipple ring doubled as a pacifier.

I also felt really mainstream driving back and forth to the March on the highway. It seemed like everybody with an identifying bumper sticker or a butch haircut was cutting each other off on the road and honking madly just to get your attention so they could wave meaningfully. I want to know how come nobody's this friendly in a lesbian bar? You walk into a bar, nobody looks at you for three hours. My whole life I've wondered where to go to meet dykes. I should have known—Route 95!

The truth is, as queers, we don't even fit into this society's conceptual framework. I'm so sick of filling out forms that ask you to select "marital status." Recently I had to fill out a form that asked for the "occupation of the head of household." How do you figure out who's the head of a lesbian household? I know I'm the butch, but I haven't made a decision in eight years.

I'm actually extremely neurotic in relationships. I suffocate people. I mother them to death. My lover Harriet and I have all these straight friends and they're always complaining about the men they're involved with: they're cold, they're rejecting, they're uncommunicative. Harriet says to me, "Why can't you be like that?"

And I'm always afraid that she's going to leave me. Like the other day, Harriet went to the refrigerator and said, "Shit! You forgot to get milk again?!" I said, "Look, let's not make this messy. I'll move out."

Relationships are not easy. Harriet and I have been together over eight years, and by this time the sex life isn't what it was. So I keep trying to jazz it up. Sometimes when we're making love, I'll put on an accent so she'll think she's with somebody new. But she complains. She says, "Look, I'm just not attracted to your grandmother."

Harriet and I decided to register as domestic partners. The most amazing thing about the process to me was how totally normal it seemed. First we called the Office of the City Clerk. The telephone recording instructed us: "For marriage license information, press 'one' now. For record room information, press 'two' now. For domestic partners information, press 'three' now." It was obvious—we were finally entitled to do something as boring as getting married or accessing records. In just another year or two they'll probably add: "For transgender license information, press 'four' now. For whip and chain registration, press 'five' now."

The truth is, you hardly get any social privileges as domes-

tic partners unless you're sick, dead, or in jail. I could visit
Harriet at Rikers Island, but we still don't even qualify to be a
team on *Family Feud*.

And what about all those old romantic songs about getting
married? You know, like:

> *Going to the chapel and we're*
> *gonna get ma-a-arried.*

Somehow, it sounds a lot less lyrical when you say:

> *Going to the Office of the City Clerk*
> *to register as domestic partners.*
> *We're number nine hundred and thirty seven;*
> *they won't tell us how many are homosexual.*

Or how about:

> *Love and domestic partnership,*
> *Love and domestic partnership*
> *Go together like no health insurance and no presents.*

As a comic, I travel around a lot and I see a lot of road signs.
And very often I see a sign that says ADOPT A HIGHWAY. When I
see this sign, I always wonder, "What if you're a lesbian? Is it
legal to adopt a highway? Isn't there a danger that somehow
you'd influence the highway and it would become a lesbian
highway?"

Actually, I was on a lesbian highway recently. I was driving in North Carolina, when all of a sudden I saw a sign that said ENTERING CHARLOTTE. Thank God, I just had time to reach into the glove compartment and grab some latex.

Some of my friends have kids, and the one thing they wish more than anything else is that their children will turn out to be less fucked up than they are. It's like our parents hoping we'd be more economically secure than they were. My mother used to say, "I was so poor that if I wanted a toy, I had to sew two buttons on a dish towel to make a doll. You don't know how fortunate you are to have everything you have." In a few more years my friends will say to their kids, "I was so fucked up that just to be functional, I had to go to group on Tuesday, individual on Thursday, and twelve-step on Monday, Wednesday, and Friday. You don't know how fortunate you are that you just call a couple of hot lines on the weekend!"

As you can tell, a lot of my friends are in therapy, and a lot of us have feminist therapists who say that women have trouble getting in touch with their anger. But one thing these therapists don't realize is that none of these women live in New York. In New York, we're all in touch with our anger.

Let's say it's a rainy day and you're coming out of the subway and somebody opens up their umbrella and it hits you on the side of the head. Now, I don't know about the rest of the country, but any New York woman is going to say, "Will you fuckin' watch what you're doing!"

But now let's say it's another rainy day and you're coming

out of the subway, only this time it's you opening up the umbrella and you hit somebody else on the side of the head. Of course, they'll say, "Will you fuckin' watch what you're doing!" And you'll say, "For Chrissake! Can't you tell it was a fuckin' accident!"

It's very easy to tell the New York dykes on vacation in Provincetown. They're the ones, if you accidentally brush against them in the water, who say, "What's the matter— ocean's not big enough for you?" There's nothing like New Yorkers relaxing on vacation.

I'm a native New Yorker, in case you couldn't tell. I grew up in a large Jewish extended family in Brooklyn in the 1960s. Who were our role models back then? Basically, Miss Jane Hathaway on *The Beverly Hillbillies.*

It was especially difficult growing up as a butch. I'll never forget the trauma of clothes shopping with my mother. I mean, Macy's, the biggest department store in the world, had no department for me. My mother used to plow through the racks in a doomed attempt to make me look like Shelley Fabares on *The Donna Reed Show.* Then we'd get home and she'd make me try on the outfits all over again and model them for her. I knew that the second I came out of my room, she'd pull out all the stops in a desperate effort to reinforce any little pathetic glimmer of femininity. Basically, she'd have a Gorgeous Attack: "Gorgeous! Gorgeous, gorgeous, gorgeous, gorgeous! Do you look gorgeous! Turn around! Gorgeous! Go upstairs and show your Aunt Gertie!"

Now, the word "gorgeous" was reserved for female attire.

If my brother Warren got a new suit, it was: "Sharp! Sharp, sharp, sharp, sharp, sharp, sharp! Do you look sharp! Turn around! Go upstairs and show your Aunt Gertie!"

So I'd go upstairs, my aunt would give me the once-over, and she'd say, "Stunning! Very, very delicate! Very, very dainty!" By this time I was so miserable that I actually heard what she said as: "Very helpless! Extremely passive! Absolutely victimized!"

Somehow, I lived through all this. Now I go to therapy so many times a week it's like I live my life in little fifty-minute intervals. And I've been talking about my family with my therapist for so long that by now she has her own problems with these people. Last week, when I was talking about my mother, she said, "Look, I don't want to hear a thing that woman has to say!"

My parents recently retired to Florida. I wanted Harriet to come with me to visit them, and I told her the best way she could survive the experience was to think of herself as an anthropologist—kind of like Zora Neale Hurston coming down from New York to observe the local folk customs in Florida. Certain observations would be obvious. Like: "Everybody talks at once here." "Food is the center of everyone's life here." "Exercise hasn't been discovered yet here."

There are basically two main topics of conversation. One is what restaurant you're going to go to for the next meal—which you discuss in the current restaurant over the current meal—

although six nights out of seven you end up at the Early Bird Special at HoHo's Kosher Cuban Chinese Dumpling House.

The other conversation is about how convenient or inconvenient everything is. Like: "You see the trash compactor, right outside our apartment? It's very convenient!" "You see our parking space? You don't even have to walk ten steps; it's so convenient!" I once pointed out to my mother that lesbians don't need birth control. Was she impressed! She said with new respect in her eyes, "Now, that's convenient!"

After the visit Harriet said that she wanted to write a book about her experiences. She's going to call it *Their Eyes Were Watching Television*.

Our better trips are to women's festivals. I love them. The first time you go to one is an especially astounding experience. You just can't believe you're with all these women. You start to bask in the sunshine. You sway to the music. You start to feel so natural. Pretty soon you fling off those unnatural, confining clothes. Your breasts are hanging free and loose. You turn to your left and you see all these wonderful, naked women and a mountain. Then you turn to your right and you see—Ms. Weber from the Personnel Department! "Oh, hi, Ms. Weber! I'll have that health insurance form on your desk Monday morning!"

We've certainly developed an alternative lesbian culture at these festivals. Where else can you go and hear over the loudspeaker, booming through the trees: "Will Running River Schwartz please meet her girlfriend Oat Bran at the light-bondage tent immediately!"

And there are always a couple of women who have their entire heads shaved except for a woman's symbol running like a trimmed hedge around the crown of their heads and down the back. And I always think to myself, "Where do these women work?" It's one of the great mysteries of life.

A friend of mine named Marsha recently had a very unexpected romantic experience at a women's festival. She's thirty-eight, and at a "Welcome the Goddess" ceremony she met a woman who turned out to be twenty-three. You know, someone who's still filled with youthful energy and enthusiasm. The first night they were together, her girlfriend said to her, "I want to be the most amazing lover you've ever had." Marsha answered, "Sure, go ahead. Try. I'm rooting for you."

If you meet a woman at a women's festival, there's an excellent chance that she's a lesbian. But it's not that way in the rest of our lives. Sometimes you meet a woman and you *think* she's a lesbian, but you're not really sure. So we have these little exchanges in code. Like you might casually say, "You know anybody driving to Provincetown this summer? With her cat?"

Or you can meet this perfectly articulate woman who you *know* has a Ph.D. in linguistics, but when you ask her "Whom do you live with?" she answers, "They're a lawyer."

Or you can be sitting around with a group of co-workers and some straight woman will say, "Did you see that new guy in the public relations department? Isn't he really cute?" And some other woman will say, "Aarrgghh!" And you say, "Aarrgghh!" And an entire conversation has just happened.

But an easier way to find out is to go to somebody's apartment, look inside her kitchen cabinet, and count how many Celestial Seasonings herbal teas she has. If there are more than six, she's probably a lesbian.

frank decaro was born in Manhattan in 1962 and grew up as an Italian Catholic only child in Little Falls, New Jersey —eighteen miles and a world away. He attended Northwestern University's Medill School of Journalism in Chicago, where he wrote "Being Frank," a biweekly column for the *Daily Northwestern*.

After graduation DeCaro worked first as an entertainment writer in Fort Collins, Colorado; then, as a menswear columnist in Detroit. Since 1988, he has written about popular culture, entertainment, fashion and design as a "special writer" for *New York Newsday*, where in January 1993 DeCaro became one of the few openly gay columnists writing about gay issues for a mainstream newspaper, with his "Frank's Place" column appearing every Tuesday.

As a freelance writer, DeCaro contributes regularly to *Esquire Gentleman* and *Out*. His work has appeared in *Martha Stewart Living, Entertainment Weekly, Mirabella, Elle, Mademoiselle, Avenue,* and *Vogue*. He is currently working on a humorous memoir entitled *A Boy Named Phyllis,* which Addison-Wesley will publish in 1996. He collects Polynesian kitsch and lives in New York City.

frank decaro

So What Constitutes a Homosexual Act?

All those afternoons I thought my father was going to OTB and stopping for Coney dogs at Libby's Luncheonette, he was really in Washington advising the Pentagon on homosexuals in the military. I mean, it *must* have been my father. His policy has *always* been "Don't ask, don't tell, don't pursue."

Since I was sixteen—the year I realized there were other teenage boys who had impure thoughts about *Starsky and Hutch* —my rule of thumb with my father has been: He doesn't ask me about my love life, I shouldn't tell him anything he doesn't want to know, and, as a good son, I mustn't pursue anyone, even if he's tall, has a good job, and my mother (a woman who once called Bill Clinton and Al Gore "a handsome couple") thinks he's cute.

Better my father's son should be "a little flaky" and "married to his job" than openly gay and single. My mother, like most mothers of gay kids, is cooler about this. The other day she told someone I haven't seen since high school, "Frank doesn't live in Manhattan; he lives in Greenwich Village."

Next, she'll be telling her friends at the Rosary Society I sing backup for Sister Sledge.

My dad, though, has always asked, "Why must your life be an open book?"—which is just another way of asking the tired question always put to gay men and lesbians: "Why should anyone know what you do in your bedroom?" Asked *that* question, I'm always perplexed. What do opening mail, talking on the phone, reading, and sleeping—the four most common bedroom activities, despite America's preoccupation with sex—have to do with being gay? Besides, no one is gay just in their bedroom.

We're gay in the kitchen, the living room, the bowling alley, the supermarket, everywhere. We're gay when we're sitting at *Coneheads* and not laughing once. Gay when we're spending $140 on a French teacup–pattern throw pillow at Bergdorf Goodman. Gay when we're playing the k.d. lang/Andy Bell remake of "Enough Is Enough" for the thirtieth time in one night. No matter what some people say, being gay is a twenty-four-hour thing, like 7-Eleven.

The new military-policy guidelines—essentially "Be all you can be . . . but in private"—don't seem to understand that. They say military personnel can be gay, but they have to be celibate and not talk about it. (Have you ever *tried* to be celibate and not talk about it? It's not easy.) This kind of yes-and-no double-talk reminds me of that joke in *Rabbit Test,* a Joan Rivers movie, where a Jewish woman asks a priest if she may enter his church. He says, "Yes, but don't pray."

With the ban eased but not lifted, servicemen and -women can have gay friends, go to gay bars, march in gay-rights parades, read gay magazines, list a same-sex someone as the person to contact in case of emergency, and the military won't investigate or discharge them. But the government draws the line at "homosexual conduct" and "homosexual acts," and it doesn't just mean doing the wild thing. It means hand-holding, dancing together, flirting, what have you.

Its definition of homosexual acts is too wide and not wide enough at the same time. Wouldn't it seem to include all those straight boys who dance together at rock concerts and all those football players who hang all over their teammates and pat their butts and such? Oh, I forgot. That kind of stuff—my dad's kind of male-bonding stuff—is OK. But air-kissing or letting a man cry on your shoulder isn't.

It's too tender.

Then again, the Pentagon's definition doesn't include some of my favorite homosexual acts: giving an elegant dinner party for twenty-three in a one-bedroom New York apartment (including flowers that are the exact same shade of cerise as the tablecloths), remembering all the words to "Down in the Depths on the 90th Floor" (and pronouncing "pailletted" correctly), doing a drop-dead, accurate impression of Diana Scarwid (who played the older Christina in *Mommie Dearest*), and arguing who aged better, David Cassidy or Bobby Sherman? That kind of thing is awfully gay to me. Certainly, my father—a World War II veteran—wouldn't understand any of it.

Maybe I'm selling my old man short, though. He did tell me he got choked up when Donahue did a show on lesbians who were discharged from the military. And maybe his suggestions of celibacy have more to do with a fear of AIDS than with any shame. When I asked him about President Clinton's compromise, Pop said he understood why "you guys want the right to do whatever you want in life," and he did say, "This thing will work itself out." Before he hung up, this man who spent his late teens in a tank destroyer in Europe—the years I discovered my way through downtown Chicago—asked me, "Why the hell would you guys want to be in the military anyway?" I didn't have an answer.

You Are What You Serve

"You know the best thing about gay people?" Louise said the other day. "It's the food."

The night before, she'd had a disastrous date with a perfectly nice heterosexual gentleman who tried to impress her with an expensive Russian dinner. "I went out for foreign food and ended up with something I could've gotten on American Airlines," she kvetched. "Then we had to go see *Tommy*. Oy!"

Louise Harris, who is Brooklyn's answer to *Tales of the City*'s Mona Ramsey, is spoiled. Not only is she a terrific cook, but most of her many gay male friends are too. They're also stylish and smart; guys who are able to wear periwinkle and spell it too. Anyway, we both subscribe to the notion that if you're going to be gay, you might as well be fabulous.

It's a birthright.

In modern times, though, as gay people have asked their straight brothers and sisters to accept diversity, we've had to acknowledge diversity ourselves. We've been forced to understand that gay people come in as many different flavors as straight people. You can be gay and still be dull or tacky or unfunny. "Of course you can," a friend said. "You've met Curtis."

In this matter I am in complete denial. I want desperately to believe—despite overwhelming evidence to the contrary—that all gay people can entertain as elegantly as Martha Stewart, dress as deliciously as the Duke of Windsor, and trade gloves-off barbs like Truman Capote going ten rounds with Gore Vidal.

Well, as they say, it ain't necessarily so.

I remember the first time I met nonfabulous gay people.

It was shattering.

The year was 1984, and although I didn't ski, hated scenery, and knew not a soul in any of the states I assume are between Chicago and Los Angeles, I moved to Fort Collins, Colorado—my first newspaper job. In the closet at the office, I wanted very much to meet other gay people in town, and I figured the best way to do this was through the gay and lesbian alliance at Colorado State University. I called them and wrangled an invitation to their next potluck dinner. It was to be a backyard affair.

Showing up late from work—where I'd spent the day trying to convince my editors that the gay band Frankie Goes to Hollywood was more relevant to the eighties than the Beach Boys—I felt sheepish. I'd only had time to pick up a couple of boxes of assorted Pepperidge Farm cookies. How embarrassing. These were for eating over the sink, not for company. Please, if my big-city friends had seen me schlepping store-boughts to a dinner party, they'd have died or killed me or both. It just wasn't done. It *was* done in Fort Collins, however.

The menu—I will never forget it—was ripe for such an

uninspired addition. Weaver's frozen fried chicken (reheated by the alliance's president) was served with a side of Rice-A-Roni made "special" by adding almonds—the treasurer's secret recipe, although not my idea of a real San Francisco treat. For dessert, a lesbian brought a watermelon in its natural state, by which I mean she had *not* carved it into a basket and filled it with melon balls, all pink and lovely and round. It was a watermelon. Period.

Anyway, someone tasted one of my cookies, which had been put on a plate—thank God—and said, "Wow, these are great! What are they!?!"

"They're Mint Milanos," I said. *"I got them at Safeway!"*

You'd have thought I invented them.

I left shortly thereafter in a panic and immediately called my most tasteful friend, Harry Althaus—an actor who can work the color teal better than anyone in Chicago—and said, "You've got to get me the [heck] out of here. These queens don't know from Mint Milanos! Mrs. Fields would kill them! I'm doomed."

Well, six months later I moved, not just because of the cookie naïveté, but partly. Oh, I did befriend three fabulous gay men in that small Colorado town. All of them have since left. One lives here in New York now, one in Los Angeles, and one in San Francisco. As the Thom McAn ads put it, we all moved to the big city to escape our unglamorous pasts. None of us have any intention of ever going back to Fort Collins. In fact, when activist friends said last summer that they were boycotting Colorado, I said, "Please, I've been boycotting it since 1985."

1997's Biggest Controversy:
Haute Crime

The winter of 1997 was a really weird time to be in New York. Women were wearing shoulder pads and floppy bows again, *Dynasty: The Next Generation* was the hot TV show, and Bill Clinton was starting his second term with as much controversy as he'd begun his first.

Keeping a promise that had helped him get reelected, the President signed an executive order mandating that openly heterosexual men be allowed to serve in all levels of the fashion industry. From runway to retail, straight men had to be accepted as equals, no matter how hopelessly, *flamingly* heterosexual they were.

Needless to say, unenlightened gay people flipped up and down Seventh Avenue.

"First, the 'hets' wanted to wear our earrings, then they wanted to wear stretchy athletic wear outside the gym. Now they want us to accept them as full-blown fashion equals? Forget it!" said a wardrobe consultant in Chelsea. "Mark my words. You give them floral ties, and let them wear vests without shirts, and they're going to want everything. We can't let this happen."

The closed-minded clothes-minded doubted the creative abilities of straight men, feeling their heterosexual counterparts were better suited to tailoring than actual designing. "Have you ever seen a straight designer's sketches?" one artist said. "My lesbian neighbor's two-year-old can draw chic-er chemises."

Some feared the increased presence of straight men in the fashion world would drag down the industry's taste level, something that gay men and straight women had worked for generations to maintain. "Oh, please. There's not a straight man alive who could even make it through platform boot camp, let alone survive season after season on the selling floor," one Madison Avenue shoe designer said. "Where do they get off wanting equality?"

Initially, top American fashion designers had urged a six-month delay so the potential impact of homo-hetero high-fashion integration could be examined. The staunchest among them suggested the creation of segregated changing rooms so gay people wouldn't feel uncomfortable. "You'll be hard-pressed to find a high-ranking gay man in fashion who will admit that he's in favor of letting avowed straight men change clothes alongside gays," one designer said. "That kind of revolution will take decades."

Opinion polls suggested that a majority of Americans felt that straight men could serve in all levels of fashion if they kept their sexual orientation a secret. But the notion that they would want to be proudly, openly straight had people freaked.

There was a sharp increase in *"haute* crimes," as *Women's Wear Daily* dubbed incidents of fashion-related straight bashing.

Banner headlines ranted GAY WILDING STALKS SEVENTH AVENUE! Things got so bad in some workrooms that heterosexual embroiderers wouldn't even utter the word "fagoting" for fear the stitchery term might be taken as a slur.

Straight worries were not unfounded.

Outside one designer showroom, a heterosexual man in a pale off-the-rack suit and a pinkie ring was thrown in the mud and taunted by several gay men in black cashmere shrieking, "Winter white is not a color, straight boy!"

At a well-known Fifty-seventh Street specialty store, three gay salesclerks jeered a straight man who had tried—unsuccessfully—to mix Gaultier and Armani pieces in the same outfit. They called him a "sartorial knuckle-dragger."

On the main floor of one department store, a melee broke out between three male fragrance models and a football player. The details are just too grisly to recount here. But, Geraldo scored some of his highest ratings ever with an hour dedicated to the incident.

In response to all the violence, straight rights groups fought back. Closeted straight men had always worked in fashion, they insisted. Some great designers had been heterosexual males. Married even! And it was true. But they had always *passed* for gay, hiding their sexual orientation by displaying sophistication and taste, good color sense, and the ability to accessorize beyond braces and cuff links. These pseudo-gays laughed when colleagues told Sandra Bernhard jokes. Some dressed so well and behaved so charmingly no one would have guessed they preferred mixed-gender relationships.

These straight men just wanted to be themselves, hetero rights advocates maintained. They wanted to serve their country's fashion needs, just like their gay brothers. They were valiant straight pioneers who realized that it would be tough at first. Integration was never easy. But they knew in their hearts that, someday, fashion wouldn't discriminate against anyone— even if they led alternative lifestyles and wore Coors beer T-shirts.

lea delaria has been a professional lesbian since 1982; before that, she freelanced. Her wry, witty, and vulgar outlook has garnered her critical acclaim, rave reviews, and an abundance of sex.

Every time Ms. DeLaria enters a stage, she discusses her queerness. Industry individuals, family, even other lesbians and gays, warn her that such behavior is career suicide. On the contrary, she has received two San Francisco Cable Car Awards, two Provincetown Golden Gull Awards, and was named one of New York City's ten funniest women by *Nitelife* magazine. She was featured on ABC's *20/20* and writes as well as performs in the PBS comedy series *The World According to Us.* Her debut music-and-comedy album, *Bulldyke in a China Shop,* is a bestseller on the Ladyslipper Music label.

Lea DeLaria's entire act is a vain and as yet unrealized attempt to impress Sigourney Weaver.

lea delaria

Ms. DeLaria's Dating
Tips for Dykes

Lesbians are terrified of sex. We just don't rock 'n' roll the way the fag boys do. Gay men go out and hump and jump and actually do things like have group sex. Can you imagine lesbian group sex? It would take three girls, two to do it and one to write a folksong about it.

Let's face it, it's fucking impossible to get a date if you're a single dyke. Why? Because lesbians go from one long-term relationship to the next long-term relationship. So if you're single, you gotta be really fast to snatch 'em in between (I choose my words very carefully). But believe me, it's not very easy to snatch 'em. Why? Because lesbians always travel in a group, always in a pack, because you never know when someone is going to throw a really good game of softball. With very few exceptions, everyone in this group is attached to someone else in this group and they are all EACH OTHER'S EX-LOVERS!! You want to say to them, "Hey, girls, why not let me put some new blood in this family. All the kids are gonna be retarded."

So for many years now it has been my sacred mission to put some new blood in the lesbian community by pointing women, as it were, down the yellow brick road toward hot dyke sex. Vaginas united will never be defeated.

I do this by answering questions about lesbian dating and sex. No question is too difficult, or situation too bizarre, because I am an expert on the subject. After all, I am the woman who got to feel Martina Navratilova's thigh at the 1993 March on Washington. It was like feeling up a Buick.

I am able to answer anything, anything at all, because I have joined the nineties and become much more spiritual and holistic, and I've had a natural crystal imbedded in my uterus. This crystal allows me to channel the energies of the universe. I call it my beaver receiver.

So let's get started right away. Here are some useful questions and answers.

Q: What do you do when you go out on a date and the woman has large breasts?
A: Suck 'em.

Q: How do you keep from sleeping with all the players on your rugby team?
A: Join a men's league.

Q: What's the best way to wipe your face after oral sex?
A: With Jodie Foster.

Q: I am a gay man with menstrual envy. When does it come? What's it like?

A: You are a very disturbed queen. When does it come? Once a month in harmony with the lunar cycle and my VISA payments. What's it like? Have you ever seen the movie *Alien?*

Q: **What do you do when you go out on a date and the woman has long fingernails?**
A: You'll probably do this. AAARRG!!!

Q: **How many times can a lesbian orgasm?**
A: As many times as she fucking wants. That's something we've got over you guys. You got the money, you rule the world, but I can cum five hundred times in an hour if I want to . . . So go ahead and keep the world.

Q: **What is the most fun method of lubricating your lover when she's dry?**
A: *(Sticks out tongue)* Wellth, leth meth sthee. Actually, I don't know much about lube. I make my own.

Q: **What do I do if my woman hates her ear tongued?**
A: Fist it.

Q: **Is lesbian dating an oxymoron?**
A: No, lesbian fashion is. OK, sure, lots of us dykes have joined the nineties with our Doc Martens boots, lipstick, and pierces. Thanks to Lesbian Chic, we dykes are now "in." I for one don't get Lesbian Chic. They take two straight women, slap lipstick on them, throw 'em on the cover of a magazine, and call it "Lesbian Chic." We are the new fashion accessory. "Ladies, don't bother with that Gucci purse—put a lesbian on

your arm!" People always say the same thing: "Lesbian Chic was started by Madonna." Well, excuse me, but could we have a lesbian start Lesbian Chic? Not that I have anything against Madonna. She can lick milk out of my bowl any day.

Q: If lesbians are so chic, how come most women loving women are dressed exactly alike?
A: Because when lesbians become lovers they turn into one and the same person. I'm going to open a store for lesbian lovers: we'll have one outfit in every size. Actually, I forget we already have that store: The Gap.

Q: What's up with "the haircut?"
A: You've all seen "the haircut." It's short on top, long in the back. I call this cut "the mud flap." Only lesbians and Billy Ray Cyrus have this haircut. This haircut is an achy-breaky-big-mistakey.

Q: Why do lesbians have earrings in their noses?
A: Because it provides an extra breathing hole for cunnilingus. Actually, I'm a little frightened by all these piercings. The whole thing could cause a lot of problems. You know how lesbians love to camp. What if you're in a tent, she has a tongue stud, you have a labia pierce, and there's an electrical storm?

Q: Is it OK to fuck your girlfriend's friends?
A: OK? Why, it's a lesbian tradition!

Q: Do lesbians use fruits and vegetables often during sex? If so, what are the most popular ones?

A: Watermelons. Well, I would say cucumbers are the most popular, but don't peel them first. They get really slippery. Whoosh . . . right out of your hands.

Q: A lot of my friends want to know what is the proper lesbian etiquette for dating a woman from one's therapy group?
A: A rather typical lesbian question, don't you think? I would say if you want to date, go ahead, and if the therapy group objects, lie to them.

Q: What if the dyke of your dreams has three breasts?
A: If you love her, you'll grow another hand.

Q: What's a girl to do when she forgets her vibrator at her lover's house a thousand miles away?
A: Buy a new one—duh! If that doesn't work, try the electric toothbrush. Don't you hate that? You're going home for Christmas or whatever and you're packing and you see the vibrator and you go, "Should I, shouldn't I, nah, I don't need it." Three days later you're in the bathroom with the electric toothbrush.

Q: I'm dating a married woman. What should we say to her husband?
A: Nannynannynannynannynanny.

Q: How do you *really* use a dental dam?
A: I assume most of you know what a dental dam is. A dental dam is lesbian safe sex. It's a little square of latex which you can

get NOWHERE. NO FUCKING WHERE! You go to these gay gatherings and they throw condoms at you by the bucket and they draw you a picture of a dental dam.

So, if you want to be safe and cannot find a dental dam, then I suggest you use Saran Wrap, which is actually better because what you don't finish you can wrap and save for later.

Q: Why are there no fun lesbian sex toys?
A: Sex is supposed to be fun. Dental dams are no fun. NO FUN. Now we know what the boys have been complaining about all those years. It must be like going down on the Michelin Man.

I say if you want to be safe and you want to be fun, there is nothing more safe and more fun than strapping on a big dick and fucking her brains out. Everybody sing: "Strap on *[clap, clap]*—Strap off *[clap, clap]*—Strap on, strap off—The Strapper!"

Good toys are hard to find, though, and I have figured out why: it's because we're lesbians. You see? No? Well . . . what is lesbianism based on? What is the very foundation upon which lesbianism is built? Sharing. That's right. Lesbianism means sharing and support. So what does a lesbian do when she wants something? She goes to a store that's *owned* by a lesbian that sells products *made* by lesbians which are *about* lesbians *for* lesbians. A lesbian will go to one of those crystalhealingsistermountainwomanrain stores, and when she gets there, she finds that the sex toy selection SUCKS! They always have *millions* of vibrators, big vibrators, small vibrators. I've got one with a snooze button. It's for those really cold mornings when you just need five more minutes.

Among all those vibrators, however, there are rarely any

dildos, and I once again have figured out why. It's because we're still lesbians. You see? No? Again? All right, it's because we are lesbians . . . and dildos . . . look . . . like a penis. ("AAAAHHH!!! DON'T PUT THAT ON, RAINBOW! IT LOOKS LIKE A PENIS!") In order to deal with this traumatic reaction, lesbian stores have come up with a plan. They sell you a dildo in the shape of a dolphin. Just who I want to be fucked by, Flipper. ("Hey, Flipper, go get Bud . . .")

I'm sorry. I just can't get into this dildo in the shape of a dolphin or a corncob or a beaver with a movable tongue. When I strap on a dick, I want it to look like a dick. Call me old-fashioned.

Q: What's your favorite position to fuck in?
A: Honey, the only time I get off my back is to get up on my hands and knees so I can get it from behind. I know I look big and butch but femme, femme, femme. I've seen more ceilings than a roofer, OK?

Q: Is there anything a penis can do that a tongue or a finger can't?
A: Well, urinate comes to mind.

Q: Have you ever been with a dyke who ejaculates?
A: Yes, I have, but you have to be careful because that shit really burns when it gets in your eyes. Matter of fact, that's what a lot of politically correct lesbians use as Mace.

Q: What can two femmes do in bed?
A: Each other's makeup.

Q: Just how responsible am I for my partner's orgasm?
A: Well, I guess that pretty much depends whether or not you're there.

Q: Jilling off? Petting the bunny? What do you call it when you masturbate?
A: I call it the end of the day.

Q: Do lesbians enjoy the sweat under their breasts as much as gay men enjoy the sweat under their balls?
A: You queens are wicked. Yes, we do; as matter of fact, we even bottle it and sell it as Miller Lite.

Q: You tell your date you're butch and she doesn't know what that means, what do you do?
A: Fuck her brains out, you got a young one!

Q: I've seen this woman I really like, but I have no idea how to approach her.
A: This is THE perfect lesbian question. Lesbians have no idea how to approach each other. If lesbians had to procreate, there would be no people in this world.

This is what lesbians do. You see this woman you like and you say to yourself, "Ooh, ooh, I really like her, I mean I REALLY like her. I like her. I like her. You know what? I like her! You know what I'm gonna do? I'm gonna get up. I'm gonna go over there and I'm gonna ask that woman to dance 'cause I like her. Yes I do, I like her. I like her. I like her. I REALLY like her . . . So I'm gonna get up . . . I'm gonna go over there and I'm gonna ask that girl to dance 'cause I like her. Yes I do, I like her. I like the way she looks, the way she's sitting over there in her little miniskirt sipping her martini. So I'm gonna get up, go over there and ask that girl to dance. Maybe we'll have two dances, three dances, four dances, maybe she'll tell me her name. We could go out on a date, this could be a relationship . . . THIS COULD BE A RELATIONSHIP! And all I have to do is GET UP, go over there and ask that girl to dance, so that's what I'm gonna do. Get up and go over and ask her to dance."

Then you go home and write about it in your journal. I know what you're afraid of. Rejection. Well, let me tell you there are two ways to handle rejection: 1) if that girl won't dance with you, it is her loss; 2) always keep your sense of humor. Keep your sense of humor especially when dealing with women because we are a pain in the ass. Believe me, sometimes I wish I was straight. You screw a guy, he falls asleep. That's it. None of this "What are you thinking?"

So when approaching a woman remember: 1) her loss 2) sense of humor. Then march right up to her and say, "Would you like to dance?" If she says no, then say, "Well then, I guess a fuck is out of the question."

emmett foster was raised in Santa Monica, California. His plans to be a Mormon missionary were abruptly changed when he discovered his homosexuality, and instead he opted for a career in the theater. After receiving his B.A. in theater from California State University, Los Angeles, Foster worked as a personal assistant to Joseph Papp at the New York Shakespeare Festival for eighteen years, until Mr. Papp's death in 1992. He is best known for his comic autobiography, *Emmett: A One Morman Show,* which was produced at the Public Theater in New York and later toured at the Zephyr Theatre in Los Angeles, the Valencia Rose and New Performance Gallery in San Francisco, and the Alice B. Theatre in Seattle. He has performed in the New York Theatre Workshop's O Solo Mio Festival and has written and performed comedy in New York venues like The Duplex, Don't Tell Mama, Westbeth Theatre Center, Mostly Magic, and Dixon Place, where he regularly develops new material. More recently he curated the annual New Works Festival for TWEED and performed at the New York Theatre Workshop as part of Gay Games IV and Cultural Festival.

emmett foster

Nelson Volunteers

(As the lights come up, Nelson is sitting at the information desk in the entrance of the Lesbian and Gay Community Services Center in New York City. He is a handsome, well-preserved forty, if a bit overmoisturized. He is generous and outgoing. We come in on a phone conversation in progress. All props and people are imagined, and much of the action is mimed without interrupting the dialogue.)

No, you cannot get it from toilet seats.

Give me your name and address and I'll send you a pamphlet. Uh-huh. Uh-huh. One-oh-oh-three-six. Okay *(waves to Charlie)*, I'll send it right off. You're welcome.

Yo, Charlie! Yolanda is pissed at you, you better watch out! You said the Men's Square Dance could have the large hall on Saturday, and the Lesbyterians have it booked for their dance. I told her that, she doesn't care. She said those queens could go do-si-do at Roseland for all she cares. She's not giving up the hall. Well, she's fuming, so beware.

(To new person) Pardon me? *(Points to board)* The schedule's on the board.

(Picks up with friend on hold) Jeff, are you there? I don't know, I guess the holidays brought it out in me, I just feel like my life is so empty. I know that doesn't make sense, because I have such good friends like you and Al and Raymond, and Lord knows I have plenty to do to keep me busy, but every once in a while I just stop and say, "What does it all mean?" I mean, yes, I'm lucky to have the inheritance, and the traveling, and I love my new penthouse, and it is gratifying the hours I put in down here. But then sometimes I just think, "So what? Where's the payoff?"

(Points to board) The schedule's on the board.

(To Jeff) A lover? Well, yes, dear, a lover would be lovely, but where is he, that's what I want to know? I mean, I'm fairly good-looking, a decent body, I've got a great personality, my cock is fine. I mean, it's average, a large average, it's a pretty cock, everybody always seems perfectly happy and satisfied with it, but . . . Hold on a sec.

(New call) Community Center Hot Line.
    No, ma'am, you cannot get AIDS from kissing, unless maybe if both parties have big, raw, open, bleeding sores in their mouths. Do you have any bleeding sores in your mouth?
    Then you're fine. *(Reads card)* "AIDS is transmitted through the exchange of blood or semen." Have you somehow never heard this information before?

Uh-huh, well, give me your name and address and I'll be happy to send you a pamphlet.

Uh-huh, uh-huh.

One-oh-oh-two-three? Fine, I'll send it out right away.

You're most welcome.

(To Jeff) Hi. Anyway, where do you find these men?

(Points far right and whispers to visitor) All the way down the hall.

(To Jeff) I mean, I socialize, go dancing on the weekends, and do the bars occasionally.

The gym? Are you joking? Everyone at the gym acts like they have a pole stuck up their ass. They never speak. I think a lot of them resent me because I never go without a trainer. But, no trainer, no incentive. *(Holds up two fingers gesturing to second floor)*

Dating?! What's that?! They have these dating workshops here, but I would never, I mean, I know HOW to date: you ask someone out, you squint over candlelight, you suffer through subtitles, and then go home and mess up my comforter. I just never could get the order of these things right. I'm too rambunctious. I always fuck first, then if they're really good, I say maybe we should go to a movie sometime. *(Waves goodbye)*

I don't know, people don't really talk much at the jerk-off clubs, and I hate the Adonis.

Oh, I think "slut" is such an ugly word. Hold on.

(New call) Community Center.

AA? Yes, we have several.

Lesbian only? All right. *(Checks schedule)*

Incest survivors? Yes, there is an "Incest Survivors" at four o'clock.

Lesbian only? All right, there's an "Incested Sisters" at seven, and a "Sappho Sisters in Sobriety" at eight, but there's no combo of AA and incest for women only.

Well, I'm sorry . . .

Yes, well . . . but . . .

Well, perhaps our five o'clock anger workshop might be more appropriate for you!

"Sappho Sisters" meets at eight in the Alice B. Room.

Well, you're very welcome!

(To Jeff) Whew! I'm back. A tough customer.

Well, I forgive her and I bless her. I'm sure her attitude was a plea for help. Give me a fucking rest! *(Points to board)*

Anyway, believe me, I'd love to meet someone at a dinner party, and get to know them, and make friends, and then have sex, but it doesn't work that way. Besides, there's never any husband material at the dinner parties I go to. The only possible husband I ever met at a dinner party was that Lawrence number, remember him? He was obsessed with me. Then I got to know him.

What was wrong with him? I never told you?

Well, a), he didn't like Streisand, even the *early* albums. And b), he was a bum fuck. And c), he was a Republican! I'm sorry, honey, three strikes and you're out!

Well, contrary to what you hear around town, I do have SOME standards. He thought because I have some money, he could talk that bigoted Republican crap to me, makes my skin crawl. Gay Republicans!? What sense does that make!? Gays for Bush? It's like cockroaches for boric acid. *(Points to board)*

Anyway, no one around here wants to have sex. They're either totally afraid of it, or they're in some goddamn twelve-step program that forbids it unless you *know* the person and *like* the person. *(Rolls eyes)* Wait a minute.

(To new person) What, sonny?

"Gay Teens"? It's not on the board? *(Checks book)* Ah, Victor/Victoria Coffee House, second floor. *(Points and watches as teen walks away)*

Jeff? God, these are children! I mean, in my day there was at least a couple years of fighting it and denial. These kids— twelve, thirteen—the first hint of puberty and they burst out of the closet: "I'm a junior faggot, where's the men?!" And some of them are really fucked up. I asked this hot little twinkie from the Bronx once, "What was your first sexual experience," and he said, "You mean other than my family?" I didn't know what to say.

Hold on.

(To new person) Kelly! How are you? Is that a machine tan or a sun tan?

Oh, were you right on the beach? Oh, I love it.

No, it's not open yet but you can leave them here. Marsha will pick them up on her way in. What is it, Louise Hay?

Oh. Well, welcome back, you look great.

Well, bring the pictures in next time. Bye, dear.

(To Jeff) Hi, that was Kelly.

Yeah, way too tan.

No, he dropped off some tapes for the bookshop.

No, he says he's over Louise Hay. These are *(looks at tapes)* Marianne Williamson.

I don't know, "A Course in Miracles." Probably teaches you how to serve a fabulous dinner party for twenty-five with one fish and a loaf of bread or something. I could give her some makeup tips.

Anyway, some people just have the knack for meeting people.

What am I looking for? What do you mean?

No. No, I don't think I'm too picky.

Well, someone who has a really sexy body but doesn't go to the gym too much. Someone who I'll never get tired of having hot sex with, it'll just keep getting better and better. Someone who loves my personality and is tickled by everything I say and do. Someone who has his own life, so I won't feel smothered by him. And someone who has his own money, so I won't wonder if he's after mine; my grandfather worked hard for my money and I'm tired of throwing it away on ingrates. But most of all, someone who will really support me in getting my cabaret act off the ground.

(Points) It's on the board!

(To Jeff) What do you mean, "unrealistic?"

Well, you asked what I was looking for. Anyway, they say that you shouldn't sit around and wait for the man of your dreams, that you should become the man of your dreams, and then you'll attract what you want. But I'll never be what I'm looking for. I think it's in the genes. I don't have that much time to spend at the gym.

(To new person) Excuse me, excuse me, there's no smoking anywhere in the building, sorry.

(To Jeff) Like last summer at the Pines, I ran into Chris Mead, and he was staying at that René Reiner's house on the beach, and everyone in that house was drop-dead gorgeous. And I thought, if only I had more time at the gym. If I had two more inches on my arms, I'd at least be invited for dinner. And with two more years with my trainer at Better Bodies, I'd be a weekend guest. None of them even spoke to me when I saw them on the ferry. But as I said, I was so lazy last year at the gym. Well, you reap what you sow, you know?

(To new person) It's on the board.

(To Jeff) No. No, I don't define myself by my physical appearance, but you can't deny that most, or a lot of, life is based on that. Hold on.

(New call) Community Center.

Gay and lesbian family picnic?

Yes, gay and lesbian parents can bring their children.

The child is gay and the parents are straight?

Well, I think if the parents and the children are both gay . . .

Well, no, straight families would be welcome. Listen, I think anyone of any persuasion, or family of any combination of persuasions, who wants to go on a picnic and have a gay old time is welcome, that's the point, it doesn't make any difference. The bus will be leaving here from the Center on Saturday morning at eight o'clock sharp, and they mean that. Seems to be quite popular, everyone always has a good time, bus full of screaming kids, it's a hoot. So tell all your friends and have fun.

You're welcome.

Anyway, Jeff, you and Al are so lucky, it solves so many problems, you have each other, and you're both negative, so you can come anywhere you want, and you've done such wonderful things with your apartment. And you never get tired or bored with him after all these years?

No, I know, I know. I know it's hard work and I'm willing to do the work, I am, but there's something wrong. Sometimes I really get to liking someone and then I lose my hard-on for them. Or they don't want me after they get to know me. I mean, I think I'm fascinating, but it seems to escape most people. It's like one always loves more than the other. *(Gestures one up and over)*

Maybe I do have that "fear of intimacy" I hear a lot about.

Oh yeah, I'm learning a lot of good stuff around here. It's good for knowing how to manipulate people. If you don't like what someone is doing, you can just say, "I have some ISSUES with this, I have to set some BOUNDARIES here," and they back right off, like magic. *(Snaps)* It's great. Hold on.

(To new person) Hi, Victor, did you get your results? How's your blood work?

Great. Well, you look fabulous.

I know, you're late. Get up there.

(To Jeff) Hi, that was Victor. He's fine, but I think he's been ill-advised on his wardrobe.

Well, he's wearing leather and chains to the "Explore Your Inner Child" workshop. I think it's a little overdressed for sharing. She is one twisted sister.

Who? Victor? I don't think so.

Yeah, he's bisexual, he goes for men AND boys.

(Gives keys) I need those back.

(To Jeff) Anyway, I've always looked for that one special person, ever since I first came out. I know he's out there, I thought I found him a few times. Donald was the first, he was so beautiful, I thought he was the love of my life. But I got so bored with the sex, the same thing over and over.

Then, when I met Bruce, I thought he was it, but then he was too boring out of bed. I need to talk to a lover, ya know, have a little intellectual stimulation.

Oh, and Patrick was the best sex of all, though I think a lot of that was the cocaine. He got so needy and crazy, I just felt smothered. He was great, though. God, he really knew about nipples. Hold on.

(New call) Community Center.

Lavender light volleyball? Hudson High School on Wednesdays at seven.

Oh no, don't worry about that. They have beginners, intermediates, and the lethal "Ultra-Violets"! You'll fit right in somewhere. Have fun.

You're welcome.

(To Jeff) Anyway, then I finally met Michael and he had everything I could want in a man. I wanted so much to be lovers, I begged him to move in and pay no rent, it was right after the inheritance, and I really wanted to spoil him, and I kept wanting more, and he wasn't willing to make more of a commitment, and he said *I* was smothering *him*. He said I didn't really love him, I was just obsessed with him. What's the difference? And he started in on this codependant/dysfunctional blah-blah-blah, so we broke up and that was bad. I was plucked. *(Whispers to co-worker)* Coffee, Sweet'n Low.

(Points) It's on the board.

(To Jeff) Then Seth came along, you remember him, what was that, '78, '79? We met at the Mineshaft and we were asked to leave because we were talking too loud about opera in the sling area. I thought he was it—it was love at first sight. He was really different. We ended up just talking all weekend. He was so cute, he meditated every morning and evening. But then the

sex turned out to be bad-bad-bad, he had no technique whatsoever. And God knows I did my best to teach him, I really did. I was so patient, I stuck it out for three months, and that's when I learned some people are just bad sex and there's nothing to be done. So, I left him. *(Winks and waves goodbye)*

Well, of course it was sad, so sad. I was very upset, you remember, I didn't go out for a couple weeks.

What do you mean? Well of course I had to leave him. I mean, what's the point? If I can't get laid, I don't want anyone hanging around ruining my sleep or monopolizing the brunch conversation. Hold on.

(New call) Hot Line.

Yes?

Well, now wait a minute. Don't do that.

What is it? Uh-huh, uh-huh, I understand.

Well, let me connect you with someone who can help you. *(Reads card)* "Don't hang up. You're not alone. I'll be off the line for just a moment, all right?" *(Pushes intercom)* Bob, pick up line three. It's important. Bob, pick up. A possible suicide, though I think he just wants to whine. Bob? You got it?

Good.

(To Jeff) Hi. Another queen going off the deep end.

Oh, something about being excommunicated from the Mormon church. Really peculiar. Wasn't even about AIDS. Speaking of these things, I still haven't been tested.

Oh, I don't know, I go back and forth. I used to just assume I had it, I mean, how could I not have it?

(Takes coffee, whispers) Oh, thank you, dear, thank you. *(Takes lid off and stirs in Sweet'n Low)*

(To Jeff) And then I think, well, maybe I *don't* have it. I know I haven't been fucked, even with a rubber, since, oh God, it's too brutal, I can't even remember how many years. I can't say I haven't had a cock or two in my mouth, which makes me a little nervous sometimes, but they say that's safe-ish now. *(Sips coffee)*

What? Where did you hear that? You can't believe everything you read. The same assholes writing these articles were the ones who a few years ago were telling you that cum was pure protein. Yeah, I really fell for that one in a big way! I felt so healthy. Hold on.

(To new person) Hi, Stewart, how ya doin'? Have you signed up for the big weekend bereavement jamboree?

Well, you better hurry up, it's filling up fast.

Good. Love the sweater, is that all cotton? Is that pink, or a peach? It's gorgeous. Are you going to Diego's funeral?

Oh, pardon me, "celebration."

What? No, no, I refuse, it's a funeral.

Well, I think it's ill-advised to have an open casket anywhere near a buffet table. Tends to put a damper on the party mood, ya know?

All right, doll, see you Thursday.

(To Jeff) Hi, I'm back. Sorry, that was Stewart, in yet another sweater.

Anyway, the hideous truth is, I haven't had sex in months.

Tell me, Madge, my pussy's twitchin'! *(Takes keys back. Becomes serious)* But there's something else going on, Jeffrey. I guess I'm getting old because, I don't know, sometimes when I get really horny, I don't even want sex after all. I really just want someone to hold me and make me feel like, oh, I don't know, like they'll be there in the morning. *(Points to board)*

Yes, yes, well, that's what I mean, that's what my shrink asked. It's a loneliness, and especially sometimes when I'm out around men, like dancing or something, and the beauties take their shirts off, it just comes over me, this intense loneliness. It's this physical thing, a feeling like there's a hole in my chest, an empty space, almost like an ache. And I feel if I can just get a hot man to have sex with, it will go away, but it *doesn't,* lately. Like the last time I went to one of Bob's safe-sex parties, I thought I had something going with this guy—we went off to be alone and we were making out, he was a great kisser—but then right after I came, he walked away. And I thought, "What was the point of that!?" And that made me real depressed, 'cause I was just as horny and just as lonely as before I went. This kind of sex is just not working for me anymore. I would just rather feel that lonely feeling than the other, horrible depression. I know I've been a big slut, but . . .

Oh, my God, hold on, royalty! Larry Kramer just walked in.

Hi, Larry. Nelson, remember?
  Yes.
  Yeah, I know ACT UP is meeting here tonight.
  Well, yes, yes, I will, I'll try.

Yes, I understand, no noise in the lobby while you're making your speech.

Yes, all right, I'll keep my eyes peeled. If any TV crews come, I'll send them directly in.

Oh, you're so right, the media is so important. What is this meeting about?

Oh, the son of a bitch. They're all bastards. Time to unleash some power!

Yes, well, yes, I'll try me best. *(Big military salute)*

(To Jeff) Whew! Who died and left her in charge of the universe?! Honey, she's draggin' out the Scud missiles tonight!

(Points) It's on the board!

(To Jeff) Well, evidently Cardinal O'Connor came out with another indictment from that sick pulpit of hers, and there's gonna be four hundred upset sissies here in a half hour. *(Cute man wanders in)* Oh, oh, oh, hold on.

(Very seductive, being as butch as possible) Hi, can I help you?

Oh, you don't need to figure out that board, it's so confusing. What exactly are you looking for?

Beginners AA? *(Checks book)* I haven't seen you around here before. Just off the sauce, huh?

Good for you, buddy. That booze can be a bitch. I never drink much myself. I try to keep everything in moderation, and I keep pretty busy at the gym and . . .

What?

Oh, I'm sorry, so sorry, of course. Oscar Wilde Room,

third floor. *(Watches him walk away, then with attitude whispers to himself)* Pardon me, I guess we're on a schedule.

(Looks disappointed) Hi. Back again. Still single.

Anyway, Jeff, maybe someday I'll figure it all out. I just wish there was someone in charge of these things who could say, "Yes, don't worry. You *will* have the great love of your life, so don't give up." Or, "No! You're *never* going to have another lover, it's not in the cards, so pack it in, girl!" Because if that's the case, I'm very good at adjusting to reality. If I knew, I could just say, "All right, fine. I can be happy and content being an old maid." Lord knows I can afford to do what I want. Spend more time at my place on St. Barts, continue to collect antiques, and do my volunteer work, and just grow old gracefully. You know the way things are going in this community, we're already something like ninety-seven in gay years. *(Points to board)*

But it is a comfort to know, Jeffrey, that if I do end up an old spinster, you know, live my life alone, that you'll be there. Because, you know, good friendships are just as hard to come by as lovers, and we've shared so much over the years. You know, I was alphabetizing my *Playbill*s last week, and do you realize we've attended thirty-seven Broadway openings? Boy, you sure got your money's worth out of that tux. Lord, we've had some fun.

Oh yeah, we've been through some shit too, we've lost some good sisters. But we definitely have some memories. Thank you, dear, and for listening to all this.

Yes, yes, I do feel better. You know I love you.

Well, thank you, darling. Listen, I'd better go fill out these room schedules before it all starts. What about this weekend?

Well, is Steven still in St. Vincent's?

Well, why don't we drop in on him Sunday morning, and then we can brunch with Raymond and Michael after.

OK, good plan. Bye, doll. *(Hangs up)*

(To new person) Yeah, the schedule's on the board. *(Sips coffee and straightens up desk as lights fade)*

marga gomez, Harlem-born and San Francisco-based, has earned a living in theater and comedy venues since the 1980s. Her stand-up has been featured on public television, A&E, VH-1, Comedy Central, and HBO's *Comic Relief VI*. Her stage background includes performances with the Tony Award–winning San Francisco Mime Troupe, the Lilith Feminist Theatre, and the groundbreaking Latino ensemble Culture Clash. In 1990 she wrote two theatrical monologues, *Memory Tricks* and *Marga Gomez Is Pretty, Witty & Gay,* which have been performed alternately at the New York Shakespeare Festival, the Whitney Museum, Montreal's Just for Laughs Festival, the Chicago International Theatre Festival, London's ICA, and the Edinburgh International Festival Fringe. Marga was commissioned by the Mark Taper Forum in Los Angeles and the New WORLD Theater at the University of Massachusetts in Amherst to write her third theatrical monologue, *A Line Around the Block*. She has also written a screen adaptation of *Memory Tricks* for *American Playhouse*.

marga gomez

From *Marga Gomez Is Pretty, Witty & Gay*

(The action takes place in Marga's bedroom the night before she is to appear on a national television talk show. There are a bed and a bedside table with a lamp, a radio, a clock, and some books.)

. . . What are Sam Nunn and General Colin Powell and all the other colons so worried about? Why can't they lift the ban on gay men and lesbians in the military? Are they afraid that millions of us will enlist? I doubt it. Don't you have to get up early there? I'll do that one day a year—for the parade. We just want the right to enlist. Like my girlfriend and I want the right to have a legal wedding. But we don't want to get married. We're queer, not crazy. Are they afraid that if we could be out in the military we wouldn't obey orders? "Company, Halt!" "No. We have to dance first." Or maybe they're afraid we won't salute anymore—just snap, "Yes, girl!"

Not that I'm pro-military, I'm anti-war. I just want to wear a sailor suit once in my life. Put a sailor suit on and go dancing for one night. White bell-bottoms are hard to find. But this will be denied me because I'm considered a deviant.

My love is deeper than the ocean, wider than the sky, and too complex to be narrowly defined. But if you must apply a label —call me a dyke, a maricona, queer, AC/DC, or an ice pick–wielding lesbian . . . but not deviant. Because that implies I'm a superfreak in bed, and I was raised Catholic. And I make love like a Catholic. Not good. With a lot of guilt. 'Cause we feel that with enough guilt there's no sin. We're still pure in the eyes of the Lord. That's what I have to tell them tomorrow. The couch potatoes. The millions of Americans who will be watching me on television with that expression on their faces, the one they use to look at queers. *(Assumes homophobic expression)*

This way no one will think that they're queer. "I'm normal, look at my face. This expression tells you that I have never had a homosexual thought and that I have never met a homosexual and if I did meet one I would run because I'm sure they would try to have sex with me."

I tried to get out of this. But there are so many of these homosexual talk shows. You dodge one and then there's: LESBIANS WITH LONG HAIR—tomorrow on *Oprah*! LESBIANS WHO HAVE NEVER BEEN ON *OPRAH*—tomorrow on *Donahue*. GAY MEN WITH ORDINARY APARTMENTS. BISEXUAL, MONOGAMOUS GRANDPARENTS. How would . . . you know?

And why are we being so unfair to straight people? Straight people can't get on talk shows anymore. No room! Straight people still have problems, don't they? HETEROSEXUAL MARRIAGES—WHY? AND WHAT ABOUT THE CHILDREN? It would be nice to share the limelight because the demand for homosexual talk-show guests is exceeding our supply. Let's face it. We breed minimally, carefully, only after much thought and couples counseling. Contrary to popular belief, we do not recruit. We can only impress.

According to the "Kinsey Report," we are only ten percent of the population. Maybe it's a higher percentage in this room. But we're being used up by these talk shows. Squeezed . . . spent. I didn't ask to do this. This was not a choice for me. It was mandatory. They had my Social Security number. This is my lesbian jury duty.

I'll serve my time to the best of my ability and, who knows, I might make a difference. To just one person. Just one. *(Pause)* That's not enough people for me to do this. I want BIG results. I want to be a role model to many lesbians, bisexuals, some gay men, and even progressive heterosexuals of Latino descent. I can do it. I just need to change my personality.

I need to be more positive and perky. *(Marga addresses imaginary television camera)* Hello, America. I love a woman, yes! A wonderful, wondrous, one-of-a-kind woman. Yes, I love a sister, a sensational, sensitive, sensuous sister. *(Pause)* Not my sister, America! Just some woman, OK? We have a marriage just like your marriage, although ours is not legally recognized. No priest performed a ceremony. We received no avocado fondue sets from our relatives. Nobody tied tin cans to the back of our car and painted JUST LESBIANS on our windshield. But in every other way, it's just like your marriages. We exchanged vows to be together until death do us part. And we have been together for five years. Five years, America. That's a long time for any marriage. We live together. We sleep in the same bed. This bed, America. *(Writhes on bed)*

And you know this bed has seen a lot of action—until about four years ago. Just like your marriages . . .

(After Marga has a confrontation with the cute young dykes who live upstairs and is left humiliated)

When did I go from positive and perky to uptight, bitter, and pathetic? I'm just like the first lesbians I ever saw. I was ten. I saw them on David Susskind's *Open End,* one of the first television talk shows. We were there. I never watched David Susskind back then, it was too dry, but my mom had it on that night. She turned down the volume very low, but I could hear David Susskind say, "Tonight's program might be offensive to people with certain religious beliefs and not suitable for children. I will be interviewing lady homosexuals." I could hear this upstairs, with my bedroom door closed and my radio blasting, because by ten I had already developed HOMOSEXUAL HEARING. I followed David Susskind's voice down the stairs into the living room and sat next to my mother on the sofa.

I made sure to put that homophobic expression on my face. So my mother wouldn't think I was mesmerized by the lady homosexuals and riveted to every word that fell from their lesbian lips. They were very depressed, very gloomy. You don't get that blue unless you've broken up with Martina.

There were three of them. All disguised in raincoats, dark glasses, wigs. It was the wigs that made me want to be one.

(Puffing on cigar, sitting with legs wide part) "Mr. Susskind, I want to thank you for having the courage to present Cherene and Millie and me on your program. Cherene and Millie and me, those aren't our real names. She's not Cherene, she's not Millie, I'm not me. Those are just our, you know, synonyms. We must cloak ourselves in a veil of secrecy or risk losing our employment as truck drivers."

(Changes to Susskind, who is also smoking) "I only hope that everyone watching will realize that you are human beings who deserve to love whomever you choose. It's really nobody's business, is it? Yes, Cherene?"

(As Cherene, smoking) "It's just that when you live in a small town, anytown, USA, then you better get used to people staring and whispering behind your back. Everybody from the bag boy at the A & P to the Avon Lady—she knows—to every neighbor in the neighborhood, 'cause the Avon Lady told them.

"Mr. Susskind. When you are in THE LIFE, such as we, it's better to live in Greenwich Village or not to live at all!

(Breaks down and snaps out of it) "At this time we want to say 'hello' to a new friend who is watching this at home with her mom on WNEW-TV in Massapequa, Long Island. Marga Gomez? Marga Gomez, welcome to the club, *cara mia.*" *(Flicks her tongue lasciviously)*

My mother was in such denial she didn't pick up on Cherene's obvious clue. Mr. Susskind and the lady homosexuals chain-smoked through the entire program. I think it was relaxing for them. I don't think they could have done it without the smokes. It was like they were in a gay bar just before last call. And all that smoke curling up made THE LIFE seem more mysterious.

THE LIFE—that's what they called it back then when you were one of us. You were in THE LIFE! It was short for THE Hard And Painful LIFE. It sounded so dramatic. I loved drama. I was in the drama club in high school. I wanted to be in THE LIFE too. But I was too young. So I did the next best thing. I asked my mother to buy me Life cereal and *Life* magazine. For Christmas, I got the game of Life.

(Smokes) And as I moved the lonely game pieces around the board, I pretended I was smoking Life cigarettes and living THE LIFE life. But by the time I was old enough, nobody called it THE LIFE anymore. Because it sounded too isolating and politically incorrect. Now we say THE COMMUNITY. THE COMMUNITY is made up of all of us who twenty years ago would have been in THE LIFE. And in THE COMMUNITY there is no smoking. *(Stamps out imaginary cigarette)*

▼

(Marga's incessant worrying leads her to her ex-Catholic schoolgirl's fear of eternal damnation for going on the talk show)

. . . God. God, this is Marga Gomez, a sinner . . . God, please don't punish me. I've suffered enough. I'll do whatever you want. What do you want? Talk to me, God, talk to me. I'll be born again. I'll tell my girlfriend, "I cannot lay with you unless you're born again, too" . . . OK, no girlfriend. I'll take unto me a husband. We'll have a Christian wedding. We'll never use birth control and I'll bear many Christian babies and they'll hate me and I'll hate them too. We'll be a typical Christian family, God, OK? We'll leave San Francisco. We'll go someplace you like, God. What do you like? Anaheim? Virginia? Just give me a sign, God.

(The upstairs neighbor's stereo is heard loudly through the ceiling)
Excuse me, I'm talking to God! The nerve. And you know what? They're gay girls up there. They should have some consideration for me. But they're cute young dykes and they don't care what I think. They are very happy about their lives. They don't know what I know! Why do they have to have fun in the building? I don't. Why can't they go out to one of their trendy, hip, au courant clubs? They have so many clubs, why don't they use them? I know where they go. They go to the G Spot, Uranus, Club Snatch, Club Clit, Club Pussy! They go to all the body parts. When I was their age, I went out every night, too. I was a regular at Club Rumors, The Hideaway, Don't Tell

Mama's, The Incognito—places you could feel proud to be a lesbian. Sounds like they're starting their own club upstairs. Club Work My Nerves!

The dykes today, who can understand them? They buy expensive Italian black leather motorcycle jackets. You know, they're at least five hundred dollars a pop. Then they go and plaster political bumper stickers all over the back of these jackets. LABIA VISIBILITY. U.S. OUT OF NORTH AMERICA. PETE WILSON IS AN ASSHOLE. Because our governor, Pete Wilson, vetoed the gay rights bill and also because he's an asshole. When we were twenty-one, we put bumper stickers on our cars, not on our jackets, because we wore down vests. Bumper stickers would pull out the feathers and then you'd have an asymmetrical down vest. Which was a fashion faux pas in the seventies. The only fashion faux pas there was in the seventies. But we expressed ourselves. We wore buttons. Political buttons, lots of them. We looked like refrigerators covered with magnets.

That's where they got the bumper sticker idea from, our confrontational, in-your-face buttons: HOW DARE YOU PRESUME I'M HETEROSEXUAL? Step back. We thought this one was so funny, remember FESBIAN LEMINIST? Get it? Don't tell me we weren't cutting edge. We paved the way for you. *(Marga jumps on bed and shouts up at neighbors)* We wore the Frye boots so you could pierce your noses today! Oh, the dykes today with their piercings! So many earrings, how can they hear? The ones upstairs have pierced their eyebrows. Oww! I can't even pluck my eyebrows. My girlfriend thinks it's a beautiful thing. She wanted us to pierce our noses so we could wear matching nose rings, like all the other couples. I said, "No, thanks, honey, I'll wear a clip-on." Now they're piercing nipples. Who started that?

(Fondling tits) Oooo, this feels great . . . Think I'll drive a spike through it! These girls are full of holes. They whistle while they work!

Since beginning his stand-up career four years ago, **frank maya** has firmly established himself as a groundbreaking performer. Maya was the first openly gay comedian to appear on MTV's *Half Hour Comedy Hour,* as well as at New York's Caroline's Comedy Club, where he headlined for twelve weeks. He has also headlined at Alan King's Toyota Comedy Festival and performed in Lincoln Center's Serious Fun! Festival. His comedy has been praised across America in publications like the *New York Times, The Village Voice,* the *New York Post, New York Newsday,* the *San Francisco Chronicle,* the *San Francisco Bay Guardian,* and *The Advocate.*

In addition, Maya performed on Comedy Central's *Out There II,* has been profiled on ABC-TV's *Day One,* appeared on ABC's *Rolonda,* and has been featured in *Entertainment Weekly.* Maya's other television credits include *The Dick Cavett Show* and *In the Life* on PBS; NBC's *Today in New York;* Comedy Central's *Short Attention Span Theater,* and CNBC's *Talk Live* and *Real Personal.*

In 1993 Maya opened his hit one-man show, *Paying for the Pool,* for a sold-out eight-week run off-Broadway at New York's Atlantic Theater.

frank maya

From *Paying for the Pool*

My Faggy Childhood

I was a very faggy little kid.

Of course *all* little boys are faggy.

You have to learn to act straight.

It's true. Watch little boys who are five or six years old. They're so silly-acting. It's a magical age, isn't it? You're running around, you're a big queen—AND YOU DON'T KNOW IT.

You're having a great time until someone tells you to stop.

My brother was very faggy and he's straight.

When we were little, his favorite thing to do was to put on my mother's red cocktail dress and run outside in the lawn sprinkler and spin around real fast. A little crew-cutted boy in a red cocktail dress spinning in the sprinkler in the sun.

Now, he's married with children.

I think they should leave little kids alone. Let them just grow up the way they want to be. Don't teach them to act straight. Don't teach them to act any way.

I have these friends who have this very faggy little son and he's so cute. And they don't mind. They're both real secure in their own sexuality, so they're not that concerned whether or not their son is gay or straight—they certainly don't care if he acts faggy. As a matter of fact, they even hired a tutor for him—this big nelly queen who spends endless hours with this little boy every day.

Anyway, this boy is SO faggy, he calls his father "Mary"! The father comes home from work and the boy walks over and says, "Oh, look at Mary, SHE'S *exhausted!* Mary, you want some coffee?"

Then he walks away, snapping his fingers.

Gym Class

Gay men are obsessed with the gym. We go day and night.

It's really strange when you think of the way we were in high school—in high school YOU COULDN'T DRAG ME INTO THE GYM.

I'm telling you, nothing could make me go through those doors.

Freshman year I started writing those notes:

Dear Gym Teacher,

 Frank is an epileptic, he has just had a heart transplant, he has cancer and he is going blind.

 Please excuse him from gym class for the next four years.

Signed,
His Mother

Now I can't stop going.

But, of course, high school was different. Especially if you were in the closet. There was all that tension in the locker room—I mean, I was so confused with all these naked guys, it was like, I wanted to suck their dicks, BUT I COULDN'T CATCH A BALL.

I knew something was off!

It's true, gay men cannot catch balls.

I don't know what it is.

I mean, once in a while you'll find a guy who can, but in general we can't catch balls.

I'm sure that's what they're doing in the military now that they can't ask—you walk in the door, they throw a ball at you and if you drop it they yell "Fag!" and tell you to get out.

The Gym

When I first went to the gym, I was a little intimidated. I went to this all-gay gym in Manhattan called Chelsea Gym. I call it "The Chelsea Re-Hag Center."

Anyway, it took me a while to get used to it.

Some of the guys there are SO big.

But it's not like they're happy, because they never think they're big enough. They're always looking in the mirror looking SO depressed and SO ridiculously big, it's like they're on PROZAC and STEROIDS.

I had a lot of trouble the first few months. I just couldn't work out. I'd go up to the gym floor, look around, and then get so intimidated that I'd spend the next hour or so downstairs in the *LOW-SELF-ESTEEM ROOM.*

Breakups

When I go through a breakup, I need to talk about it—constantly. I call my friends, I make *them* talk about it. I'd like to watch *Nightline* and hear Ted Koppel talk about it: Frank's Breakup. I want people to call in so that somehow I can figure out what the hell happened.

I wish they'd invent a boyfriend patch. You put it on your arm and you forget about the guy in two weeks.

And no matter how bad my relationship is, I always want to stay in it, I'm always working on it, I never wanta break up. If I was dating Hitler, I wouldn't want to break up, I'd be telling my friends, "Oh, he's different at home, he's so funny when we're together, he's nicer than you think." And my friends'd be like, "BUT HE'S HITLER! He's gonna destroy the world."

And I'd say, "No, he's just kidding."

I'd be looking for his inner child or some shit. I mean, DEEP INSIDE I suppose there's good in everyone, but I'm not dating the inner child, I'm dating the OUTER ADULT, who is really messed up.

I know some people don't get this inner child stuff, but it's simple: Your inner child is *you* when you were little, like around six years old, BEFORE YOU BECAME A BITTER EVIL QUEEN.

Did Your Parents Explain Gay Sex to You?

Gay sex is so confusing.

And we've always had to put up with so many rumors about it. Like this gerbil thing. I go around the country and people actually believe this rumor—that gay men like to put gerbils up their ass for fun.

Oh yeah, I *love* to put gerbils up my ass. Sometimes I go

through thirty or forty a week. I walk into the pet store and they all yell, "Nooooooo! Get a dog!"

Bad Kissers

You know, sex is nothing unless the person knows how to kiss.

Isn't that true?

I could just kiss for hours and hours, but I just can't believe how many people don't know how to do it.

I used to think you could teach someone to kiss.

You can't.

The world is divided into bad kissers and good kissers.

If your lover is a bad kisser, put a pillow over their head tonight. Otherwise you'll be on heroin in two years—shooting up pretending you love their kisses.

I went out with this guy, I was so excited, I couldn't wait to kiss him.

But unfortunately he turned out to be my least favorite type kisser—what I call the baby-turkey-in-the-rain-type-kisser.

You know what baby turkeys do in the rain?

They open their mouths, their tongues retract, and they swallow water until they drown.

They're really stupid.

Well, this guy was the exact same way.

I go to kiss him, I touch his head, suddenly his eyes roll

back, his tongue retracts, and his head goes back like it had a hinge on it.

I'm looking into his mouth thinking, "What happened? Did he have a stroke?"

It was like kissing a PEZ dispenser.

Then there are the alien-type kissers, the ones whose mouths get really hard.

They get really hot and their mouth turns into this tight, hard circle, then suddenly they lock on and you can't breathe. It's like they're trying to suck the very life out of you.

GET OFF!

Then there are the snake-type kissers, the ones whose tongues get really hard and pointy, and they start darting it in and out of your mouth REAL FAST, and at the same time it's like they're spitting at you.

It's like you're making out with a Water Pik.

I mean, your teeth look great when they're done, but otherwise, IT'S DISGUSTING.

Cats and Sex

You know what really scares me? People who cum too fast.

I went out with this one guy, he came so fast I couldn't get in the bedroom—I couldn't even get my clothes off. Plus, he had cats. Cats and sex are such a gross combination.

He had two cats and he'd let them sit on the bed, and the

trouble is cats are so judgmental. They sit there during sex, making faces, making you feel terrible. I was like, "Could you please lock those cats in the bathroom while we're having sex?"

He was outraged. "How mean! You really expect me to lock them in the bathroom all that time?"

"Five minutes?" I thought. "They can't stay in the bathroom for *FIVE MINUTES?*"

Phone Sex

And what about phone sex? Is that an alternative?

To me it seems so desperate and lonely, but I guess if you have nothing better to do . . .

Actually, I like it.

But I just wanta say one thing: Phone sex and Call Waiting are a dangerous combination.

Please choose one or the other.

I was having phone sex one night, I was really getting into it, having a great time—it was eleven o'clock at night—suddenly the beeper goes off, I pick it up, it's my mother!

She was like, "Hi, honey, what's up?"

She was depressed, she wanted to talk.

I didn't know what to do. I was naked. I was horny. And you know, when you're about to have an orgasm, you're so rude, so I said, "Mom, I'll have to call you back tomorrow."

And I pushed that button, NOT QUITE HARD

ENOUGH, and I think I'm back on the phone sex line and I'm going, "Oh yeah, I'm really hot, I'm really hot, YEAH, what are you wearing, WHAT ARE YOU WEARING?"

And I hear mother say, "I'm in my print nightgown!"

AND I CAME.

For thirteen years **steve moore** has been performing stand-up across America in clubs like The Comedy Store and The Improv in Los Angeles, Catch a Rising Star in New York, and Zanie's in Chicago. In addition, he has opened for celebrities like Dolly Parton and Joan Rivers. Recent appearances include Comedy Central's *Out There,* Roseanne's HBO special, Montreal's Just for Laughs Festival, A&E's *Evening at the Improv,* and in February 1994 Moore traveled to Australia for that country's first-ever lesbian and gay comedy festival. Diagnosed as HIV-positive in 1989, Moore has continued to tour the country entertaining and educating America as the only openly HIV-positive comedian. Currently he is at work on his autobiography.

steve moore

AIDS—God, I Hope I Never Get That Again!

I'm a bitter old queen; don't mess with me. I'm just kidding. I'm not *that* bitter.

I'll be forty in June. That's a hundred and thirty in gay years. I feel like a sugar daddy without cash. I'm trying hard to stay in shape. I rented the Marky Mark exercise video thinking that would motivate me and snap me into shape. Seemed like a good idea. The problem is that during the third sit-up, I started masturbating. Of course, after that I have to smoke a cigarette and have a nap!

I had sex in October. 1983. I did. He whispered in my ear, "Talk dirty to me . . . Talk dirty to me." I didn't know what to say. I looked him right in the face and said, "Your apartment is filthy!"

▼

I'll share with you. I go to therapy. You people can't hurt me. I'm a "dominate bottom." That means I'm a big girl, but I'll fuck you if I have to.

Thank God *Time* magazine came out with an article saying that we're gay because we have a small gland in the back of our heads. That takes the pressure and guilt off of our parents. The problem is there's not one gay man in this world that will admit to having a small gland.

I quit drinking about three years ago. I started drinking a lot because I was lonely. Now I'm still lonely. I'm just really aware of it!

Have y'all seen the gay weatherman in West Hollywood on public access Channel 97? He comes on and says:

> Hi, this is Lance Prance with the weather coming to you from West Hollywood, California.
> Christ, Southern California just had another earthquake. This one measured 6.7 on the rectum scale! Anything over 6 is a disaster. Mercy!
> I see in the Midwest we're having tornadoes. Honey,

you better click those pumps and get the hell out of Kansas . . .

Of course, down in Malibu they're having those mud slides. Whoever wrote that song, "It Never Rains in Southern California," should be slapped!

Of course, down in Phoenix it's 175°. Christ, you better just stay home, bake a quiche, have a dry martini, and listen to some old Judy Garland albums.

Oh, here's a tip. I bought some Crisco the other day. You know what I found out? That stuff is great for frying chicken. It is!

This has been Lance Prance with the weather coming to you live from West Hollywood, California, where the crosswalks say . . . ssssStop!

Now, lesbians wouldn't have somebody like that on TV representing them. I love lesbians. You've heard of "fag hags"? I'm a "dike-likee"! Actually, I've been married to a lesbian for fourteen years. I'd like to say that she's more of a man than I'll ever be and I wear the dresses in this family.

There are advantages to being married to a lesbian. We wear the same size flannel shirts. I've turned her on to Judy Garland; she's turned me on to Elvis.

The first time Wilma and Skeets—my Southern Baptist parents—met my lesbian wife, they were a little shocked. She's a very attractive woman and I had to say, "Mom, Dad, this is my wife Lois and her lover Bridgett."

Lois and I took my dad to a gay restaurant and had a pleasant lunch. My dad seemed OK and didn't realize it was a gay establishment. Later I said, "You know, Skeets, that was a gay restaurant?" He said, "Well, the food was good. One of the best cheeseburgers I've ever had!"

My parents' vacation to L.A. was a success, and they truly enjoyed my lovely lesbian wife's company. By the end of the week, my mom was saying things like, "Men are pigs; men are pigs; men are pigs." My father actually said to me, "You know, me and your wife Lois have something in common . . . We both like to eat pussy!" Talk about bonding with the in-laws!

I found out I was HIV-positive five years ago. It's been hard for me, but imagine my parents in Virginia when I had to explain to them that we're Haitian. It's been very difficult.

My parents think HIV stands for Homosexuals In Virginia. They don't know.

My friends try to console me. I always hear things like "Well, Steve, none of us ever know. I mean . . . I could be hit by a car tomorrow . . ." I always say, "Yeah, and you *will* the minute I get behind the wheel!"

My best friend gets overly protective. Every time I catch a cold, he starts crocheting a quilt. It can get ugly.

▼

People say, "Steve, you look so good I can't believe you've been exposed to the AIDS virus, you've never looked better." I figure pretty soon I'll be drop-dead gorgeous!

There are *some* advantages to being HIV-positive. You can call in sick to work and they don't ask any questions. At least now other comedians can't steal my jokes, and if they do . . . God bless them.

I hear Steven Spielberg is doing a movie about a stand-up comic who is HIV-positive. I guess he's gone from *E.T.* to AZT!

I always hear "Steve, how can you make fun of the AIDS virus? That's so cold!" I explain to them that I've been a comic for fifteen years and quite honestly . . . I don't have any other skills. Now that the Judds have broken up because Mama Judd has chronic hepatitis, I'm thinking I should give her a call. Maybe we could do an act together. We could call it "Sick and Tired."

I was home over the holidays. I'm trying to educate my parents. I explained to them that I don't have AIDS. I'm just HIV-positive and actually I'm quite healthy. Of course, then I got a Christmas card from Dr. Kevorkian.

I always say things like "AIDS—God, I hope I never get that again! It was awful; be careful out there."

It can get very quiet sometimes when I'm playing a straight club. I tend to mess with people more. I'll say things like "Excuse me, Goober, could I have a sip of your beer?" Or if it gets real quiet, I'll just say, "Don't mess with me! I could open a vein and take out the entire front row!"

My mom scolds me, "Steve, don't talk about dumping blood on people and killin' them . . . It's just mean! Now, you look good and people seem to like you, now if you'd just talk about something funny!" Like her.

One time, when I was living in a trailer in the Blue Ridge Mountains, I was taking AZT. It made me tired, nauseous, and unmotivated. My doctor said I could smoke pot to curb my nausea. When my parents found out how much I had to pay for pot, my dad, who had worked in a tobacco company for forty-two years, purchased three large pots and plant lights. There was my dad secretly growing marijuana for me in their basement. I went home Christmas Eve and there was the harvest. My mom says, "You know, I don't like the taste of alcohol and I need something to make me relax late at night. Roll some of that shit up and I'll smoke it!"

So I roll twenty-three, twenty-four joints. They say it takes a lot the first time, and I'm taking no chances. Skeets, Wilma, and myself are now in the basement throwing darts after smoking five or six joints. Suddenly the weed hits my dad and he starts breathing, or I should say gasping, for air, taking quick, tiny breaths, pointing to his chest and saying, "I can't breathe; I can't breathe right here; I can't breathe right here!" I start saying, "Dad, use your nose, for Christ's sake! Use your nose!!!"

All of sudden it hits Wilma. She starts laughing in a very high-pitched cackle, acting as if she were on acid 'cause in her mind—dope or acid—it's all the same. She starts throwing darts all over the house—through her legs, on the ceiling—shouting, "Lord, I'm up on cloud nine. Skeets, I wish you were up here with me, we could have some fun. Give me another hit of that pot."

The more Wilma cackles and sings made-up show tunes, the more paranoid Skeets gets. Next thing you know, Wilma's got cotton mouth and starts smacking her lips, "Ooh, ooh, my mouth tastes funny!" As she reaches in her purse, she says, "Ooh, I better have some breath spray!"

Immediately after she sprays her mouth, Wilma starts coughing and spitting and yelling, "Ooh, this stuff tastes like shit! Steve, would you like some?" She hands the bottle to me, and it was eyeglass cleaner. The next day my dad says, "You be sure and take that marrawanna stuff back up to the trailer. I'm afraid Wilma's gonna Windex her teeth again."

Now, I'm from the South and people all over this country accuse us Southerners of speaking funny, using words you Yankees (that includes California) never heard before. I think that shows our creative side. Take Wilma. I call what she says "Wilma-issums."

For example, she says, "Now, during sex, the vagenda . . ." I say, "Mom, it's vagina." To this day when I call her, I always say, "Hey, Wilma, what's going on? What's on the vagenda?"

Another of my favorites is when she'll say, "Your brother won't pay his light bill, but he'll go to that fancy party and rent a damn tuck!" "Mom, a tuck is a medicated pad for your butt." "Well, you know what I mean. I need a nerve pill!"

I enrolled myself in a study where I had to give myself shots three times a week for two years. My biggest fears are needles. The only way I could give myself a shot was to strip down completely naked, put a gardenia in my hair, put on an old Billie Holliday album, and sit on the toilet . . . *Don't* picture it!

I figure you have to have a sense of humor about everything. That's how I deal with my situation. In my group therapy there's a woman with breast cancer who just had a mastectomy. Everyone in the group goes for that victim thing: "Are you OK? Can I get you anything?" I'm like: "Hey, Nancy . . . Nice tit!" She laughed. My T-cells went up. It was a lovely afternoon.

KEEP LAUGHING   SILENCE = DEATH

planet q was founded in New York in 1991 by producer Michael Hyman, a cockeyed California optimist whose dream was to find the funniest dykes and fags he could to create a hilarious, cutting-edge band of queer merrymakers. Many auditions later, Planet Q premiered in October 1992 at New York's Angelika Film Center with *Planet Q . . . Live!,* a mixture of film and improv.

Switching gears in 1993, Hyman, along with founding member and director Chrisanne Eastwood, transformed Planet Q into a live-sketch comedy troupe, producing a six-month sold-out run of *Homo Alone: Lost in Colorado,* beginning in February 1993.

In August 1993 Planet Q's ownership shifted to Ann Stengel of AMS Productions, who produced in September 1993 *Yabba Dabba Q: Still Havin' a Gay Ol' Time,* which garnered rave reviews from the mainstream press ("The kind of people you want to bring home to mother . . . Delightfully silly" —*New York Times*). In May 1994 her *History of the World: Part Q* opened at the historic Courtyard Playhouse in New York's Greenwich Village.

Planet Q has appeared as a whole or in part on Howard Stern's national radio show, CNBC's *Real Personal, The Barry Z Show, Party Talk,* and various special events in and around New York City. The Planet Q ensemble features Chrisanne Eastwood, Elizabeth Hylton, Mischa Kischkum, Eric Rockwell, Daniel Ruth, Ann Stengel, and David Weincek.

planet q

Lesbian Jeopardy!

by Ann Stengel

VOICE-OVER: Welcome to *Lesbian Jeopardy!*

ALEXIS: Good evening, I'm Alexis Tribeca. Welcome to *Lesbian Jeopardy!* Our categories for this evening are:

EASY WOMEN   SOFTBALL   k.d. lang HITS   MARTINA'S EX'S

TREVOR: Excuse me *(raises hand),* is this not "Thespian Jeopardy"?

ALEXIS: *(Sarcastically)* No! Terry, you won the toss backstage, you begin.

TERRY: I'll take EASY WOMEN for $100.

ALEXIS: She has slept with everyone you know, and some you don't know.

TERRY: *(Buzz)* Who is my ex-lover?

ALEXIS: Correct, continue.

TERRY: EASY WOMEN for $200.

ALEXIS: Her easy-to-open head made her the "Butt" of jokes.

MARSHA: *(Buzz)* Who is Mary Jo Buttafuoco?

ALEXIS: Correct, continue.

MARSHA: I'll take SOFTBALL for $200.

ALEXIS: Rosie O'Donnell, Madonna, and Geena Davis.

TREVOR: What is a disgusting ménage à trois?

ALEXIS: *(Annoyed)* No! Incorrect.

MARSHA: *(Buzz)* What is *A League of Their Own?*

ALEXIS: Correct, continue.

MARSHA: SOFTBALL for $400.

ALEXIS: The face mask.

TREVOR: *(Buzz)* What is the most important purchase at the Clinique Counter?

ALEXIS: No!

TERRY: *(Buzz)* What is the piece of equipment you immediately put on when you're at softball practice and you see the woman you slept with when your lover was out of town on business?

ALEXIS: That is correct, continue.

TERRY: MARTINA'S EX'S for $400.

ALEXIS: She came out of her Ruby Fruit Jungle with Venus Envy.

MARSHA: *(Buzz)* Who is Rita Mae Brown?

ALEXIS: Correct, continue.

MARSHA: k.d. lang HITS for $300.

ALEXIS: A "perpetual" number one for eight weeks on the chart.

TREVOR: *(Buzz)* What is "It's Raining Men"?

WOMEN: No!

TERRY: What is "Constant Craving"?

ALEXIS: Correct. *(Ding-ding-ding bell is heard)* It's time to take a break and meet our contestants. *(Excited)* Let's say hello to Marsha Simon, a lesbian physical trainer from New York City who loves pizza. Tell us, Marsha, what does a lesbian physical trainer do?

MARSHA: *(Flirting)* Well, Alexis, there are so many straight women unsure of what they really want—sexually, that is. It's my job to train those women and make them into the true lesbians they've always fantasized about being.

ALEXIS: Sounds great! Our next contestant, Trevor Green, a real estate agent from Fire Island who loves dancing. *(Bored)* Hello, Trevor.

TREVOR: Hi. You know, Alexis, I'm really confused. My boyfriend told me this was "Thespian Jeopardy." If I knew . . .

ALEXIS: *(Cuts him off)* Good, Trevor. *(Excited)* And our last contestant, Terry Daniels, a femmy-butch from Queens. She's never played softball, and she can't drive a stick shift. Is she really a lesbian? Ha, ha. Hi, Terry.

TERRY: Hi, Alexis. I have three cats AND a subscription to *Sappho's Isle*. I AM a lesbian.

ALEXIS: Hey, lighten up, it's only a game. OK, now it's time for our final *Lesbian Jeopardy!* category: FAMOUS COUPLES WHO SHOULD NOT BE MARRIED. (Lesbian Jeopardy! *music*) As our lesbians are making their wagers, we'd like to thank our loser, Trevor. Thank you for wasting my . . . I mean, thank you for playing *Lesbian Jeopardy!* Please stand in the loser's corner. So Marsha and Terry are tied with $800 each. OK, Terry how much did you wager?

TERRY: I bet $800. *(Shows her answer card)* "Who is Richard Gere and Cindy Crawford?"

ALEXIS: That is correct. That puts you in the lead with $1,600. OK, Marsha, you have $800, let's see what you bet.

MARSHA: I bet $800 also. *(Shows her answer card)* "Who is Whitney Houston and Bobby Brown?"

ALEXIS: That's correct too. That brings you up to $1,600. That means you both have won today. Lesbians are so smart. Thank you and goodbye from *Lesbian Jeopardy!*

Life with Leviticus

by Chrisanne Eastwood

(Lights up on Leviticus, biblical author, busily writing at his desk and humming to himself—perhaps his haftarah or selections from Fiddler on the Roof? *Enter Aaron, carrying a bag of groceries.)*

AARON: Leviticus! Leviticus?

LEVITICUS: Shhh! Just a minute . . . I'm almost through.

AARON: I've got pita and hummus and there was a sale on . . .

LEVITICUS: Just shut up. I gotta finish this by six or God will have my head on a platter. *(Aaron is miffed)* There . . . I'm finished. Now how about a great big kiss? I'll part your red sea for you!

AARON: That line's so old, it bombed in Paradise.

LEVITICUS: Look, I've been writing this Old Testament. I'm trying to get the job editing the New Testament—if there is one.

AARON: Christ! You know there'll be one.

LEVITICUS: I'll dedicate it to you, even though you are still married to your wife. To you, my lover, Aaron.

AARON: Aw, all right. *(Kiss, kiss, kiss)*

LEVITICUS: So how long can you stay?

AARON: I told my wife I was at a tent meeting until nine.

LEVITICUS: Great! God won't send Deuteronomy until next week. I'm yours. *(Lev starts to chase Aaron around the desk. Ad-libs "I'm gonna getcha, c'mere," etc.)*

BOTH: LET ME SPIN YOUR DREIDEL!!

AARON: I'll start dinner. Can you believe that smoked goat is up to five drachmas?

LEVITICUS: "Milk and Honey"?

AARON: Yes?

LEVITICUS: Where were you last night?

AARON: Last night? Oh, I was home helping little Benjamin study for his bar mitzvah. His haftarah is really hard.

LEVITICUS: Really? Your wife said you were at an emergency tent meeting.

AARON: Oh, last night! That's right. I *was* at a tent meeting. Jebediah was speaking on some burning bush issues. Slipped my mind.

LEVITICUS: I sent a messenger to the tent. You weren't there. No one was there.

AARON: Uh . . . uh . . . meeting broke up on account . . . of . . . of flood.

LEVITICUS: There was no flood last night.

AARON: I mean pestilence . . . yeah . . . pestilence. You know how nasty that is. Sent us scattering.

LEVITICUS: Liar! There was no pestilence. There was no flood! There was no angel on high, no high boat to Sinai. You're lying to me like you lied to your wife. You're begatting with Joshua.

AARON: Joshua who? Oh, you mean that stonecutter with the pillared forearms and the finely chiseled butt? I hardly know him.

LEVITICUS: Bitch, you're lying with me! I saw you at the wishing well with him. He was holding your dipper and he didn't look too thirsty to me!

AARON: That wasn't me! I was at the well to . . . ask for directions. Joshua was there, helping me. He used the dipper to draw a map . . .

LEVITICUS: Were you coming or going, you three-timing star-shtupper? You're lying to me! I should have known. Your eyes have been wandering longer than the Israelites. I can't trust anyone who lies.

AARON: I lie to my wife to be with you!

LEVITICUS: Sure, you lie to your woman, but don't lie to a man like that! Now get out!

AARON: Fine, I'm leaving. And I'm taking my smoked goat with me, five drachmas a cubit . . . *(Exits)*

LEVITICUS: That bastard! No man is going to lie to me again. There oughta be a law against it. Wait a minute! I'm transcribing God's law, aren't I? I'll put it in the Bible. *(Scribble, scribble)* There *(reading)*: "Thou shall not lie with a man as one lies with a woman. That is an abomination!" Now about that clam that keeps repeating on me. I hate shellfish too. Here's a little ditty about shellfish . . .

Lesbian Bed Death

by Chrisanne Eastwood

(Kathy and Elaine, a lesbian couple, are in bed ready for sleep. Kathy is reading.)

ELAINE: What are you reading?

KATHY: Oh, I'm reading *Desert Hearts* again.

ELAINE: Again? Remember when we saw the movie?

KATHY: Yeah, we got so excited we had to go to the car for ten minutes.

ELAINE: We sure could do a lot in ten minutes.

KATHY: Remember the time we did it on that flight to Brussels?

ELAINE: That night!

KATHY: That flight attendant!

BOTH: Jean Louise!

ELAINE: Her breasts could save a troop of Girl Scouts in a flood.

KATHY: Yeah. Kinda like yours. *(They lean in and kiss)*

ELAINE: *(Breaks off abruptly)* Yeah, well, we were a lot less busy then.

KATHY: And younger too. Got a meeting in the morning. 'Night, sweetie.

ELAINE: My sinuses are clogged. 'Night.

(They sleep. Enter Sarah Gilbert)

SARAH: What you have just witnessed is the beginning of the end of a three-year lesbian relationship. Although Kathy and Elaine may not be ready to admit it, their sex lives are being slowly, yet painlessly eaten away by a silent killer that is creeping into bedrooms from Northampton to Santa Cruz. Normally healthy, sexually active lesbians are going to bed . . . and going to sleep.

KATHY: Who are you?

ELAINE: And what are you doing in our bedroom?

SARAH: Hi, I'm Sarah Gilbert of *Roseanne*. I'm not a lesbian, but I play one on TV. I came to talk about one of the most deadly, but little-known killers in our society, Lesbian Bed Death.

BOTH: Oh my!

SARAH: Lesbian Bed Death is an asymptomatic paralysis of a lesbian couple's sex life. You just don't do it like you used to.

KATHY: Who let you in here?

SARAH: Lesbian Bed Death, or LBD, sends approximately sixty percent of lesbians into couples counseling at one or more times during a relationship. No single cause has been isolated at the present time, but working round the clock on a cure are doctors, psychic herbalists, and folk singers.

ELAINE: You mean there's a reason why we haven't had sex? Is it a disease?

SARAH: No, it's not a disease—it's a condition. It's Lesbian Bed Death.

KATHY: Is there help for us, Sarah?

SARAH: Yes, there's help and there's hope. One thing we need to remember is this: the vagina is, and always will be, our friend. If you're nice to your friends, they will come. That is why we here at Time-Life feel compelled to offer you the five-part video series. *(Sarah presents kit to couple)*

A Lesbian Bed Death Self-help Healing Guide:
The Road to Clitopia.

This exciting multimedia package contains videos, cassettes, and an instructional handbook designed to help lesbians cope with, and eventually overcome, Lesbian Bed Death. We'll bring lesbian beds to life: L'Chaim!

KATHY: We were skeptical at first until we discovered that each video contained actual conversations and testimonials by former LBD sufferers who are now leading productive sex lives thanks to the *Road to Clitopia* program.

ELAINE: You'd be surprised to see who had the courage to speak out. Did you know that Urvashi Vaid and Kate Clinton once went almost eight months without cunnilingus?

KATHY: No, I didn't.

ELAINE: Well, it's right here in the first video, "Celebrities Share, Celebrities Dare." Knowing that you are not alone helps make the coping so much easier.

SARAH: That's right, Elaine. And the exciting video series does not stop there. You'll also receive a detailed how-to video exploring various hands-on techniques for applying sexual CPR to your DOA love life.

KATHY: And all the games were really fun too. Taped workshops led by Lindsay Wagner and Stephanie Zimbalist taught us super activities such as Sexual Role-Playing, Naming Your Breasts,

Your Body-as-a-Control-Panel-on-an-Airplane, Body Braille, and Making Music with Your Vagina.

ELAINE: Wow, let me see!

KATHY: Aside from the videos is what I feel to be the most important part of this package: the instructional handbook.

SARAH: The Time-Life program provides pages and pages of testimonials, instructions, helpful hints, holistic remedies, erotic stories, seductive pictures, graphs, pie graphs, statistics, easy-to-remove transparencies, a coloring book, and crosswords.

ELAINE: All designed in a scratch-'n'-sniff motif. A relief from those cheap over-the-counter methods that tend to leave those with sexy snouts high and dry.

SARAH: Included in the comprehensive scratch-'n'-sniff section is a complete collection of underwear samples from the LPGA tour.

KATHY: But if you're a tennis fan, take heart. If you order now, you will receive as a bonus a scratch-'n'-sniff sample from Martina Navratilova's Wimbledon Collection.

ELAINE: This is a fun section to go through . . . together.

SARAH: Everything is fun to go through together. So order now. No one has to suffer from LBD.

ELAINE: What's that number again?

KATHY: Who needs the number! I have the book right here. Let's try lesson one: "Naming Your Breasts." How about Betty and Wilma?

ELAINE: Let's try "Using Your Breasts as a Facial Massage."

SARAH: See all the fun they are having? You could have it, too, if you order now. Our operators are standing by, they're all wet and waiting. So call now!

KATHY: *(On the phone)* Is your name *really* Jean Louise?

SARAH: Call now and charge it! If you don't come within thirty minutes, you can return it. Remember, with the help of Time-Life's *Road to Clitopia,* you can take your lover's breasts into your own hands.

pomo afro homos (Postmodern African-American Homosexuals) is a Black gay male performance group based in San Francisco. Their first show, *Fierce Love: Stories from Black Gay Life,* premiered at Josie's Cabaret (San Francisco's home for lesbian and gay comics) in January 1991 and became an immediate hit, wowing audiences with its razor-sharp writing, jazzy performances, and hip-hop sensibility. *Fierce Love* and the company's second work, *Dark Fruit,* have played to packed houses across the United States, Canada, and Europe, challenging audiences from Anchorage, Alaska, to Glasgow, Scotland, to New York City and Atlanta, Georgia, to explore the contradictions, joys, and pains of Black gay life in America.

"QVC/Queer Value Channel" was staged for *Out There,* Comedy Central's first-ever lesbian/gay comedy special, with Eric Gupton as Jamal, Brian Freeman as Roland, Marvin White as Tre (and as Kiki, the "Carol Merrill" style product model), and with Joan Jett Black as Taekwanda, the fierce Black drag queen.

"Towards a Black Queer Rhythm Nation" is excerpted from *Fierce Love* and performed by the original company of Brian Freeman as the Kid, Djola Bernard Branner as the Dance-hall Diva, and Eric Gupton as the Street Kid.

pomo afro homos

QVC/Queer Value Channel

by Brian Freeman

(Two Black gay pitchmen dressed very queer contemporary sit in chairs, side by side, as if facing a camera. Kiki, a "Carol Merrill" style model, displays the products as they are announced)

TOGETHER: Lift every voice and sing
            'Til earth and heaven ring!

JAMAL: Liberty, let freedom ring!

ROLAND: Freedom Rings! *(They spin their Freedom Rings)* Our first product here today on QVC.

TOGETHER: The Queer Value Channel!

JAMAL: That's 1-800-W-O-O-R-K-I-T.

ROLAND: These handcrafted rings are available in copper, aluminum, and "diamondnesse."

JAMAL: Roland, I got two in the "diamondnesse" myself.

ROLAND: You go, boy! Because they are going fast. That's item number Q-68.

JAMAL: Buy one, we'll owe you one.

ROLAND: Jamal, these rings are such a good reminder that we have struggled for the right . . .

JAMAL: To *shop*—twenty-four hours a day, seven days a week!

ROLAND: Right here on QVC!

TOGETHER: The Queer Value Channel.

JAMAL: And speaking of values, sisters, loosen those dreads.

ROLAND: Let 'em loose.

JAMAL: And "come out"—with those charge cards!

ROLAND: Whip 'em out. Whip 'em.

JAMAL: Because you are going to love this next item.

ROLAND: Item number Q-456, we call it the Alice Walker Kit.

TOGETHER: Do you love it? I love it! Don't you love it? They love it!

JAMAL: The Alice Walker Kit starts with this handsome purple backpack.

ROLAND: Assembled by union lesbians in Berkeley, California.

JAMAL: Notice the kinte cloth trim.

ROLAND: Incorporating traditional Africanish elements.

JAMAL: And we have stuffed it.

(They gesture to the bag like stuffing a chicken)

ROLAND: Stuffed it.

TOGETHER: Stuffed it!

JAMAL: With Alice Walker memorabilia.

ROLAND: Purple candles. Purple incense. Purple Birkenstocks. Purple dental dams.

TOGETHER: Mmmmm!!! And more!

JAMAL: Order now and we'll include a free Tracy Chapman CD.

ROLAND: She's got a fast car.

JAMAL: Can we take a call?

CALLER *(offstage):* Hey, Jamal! Hey, Roland!

TOGETHER: Hey!

CALLER: This is Tre.

TOGETHER: Hey, Tre!

CALLER: Hey! I love the show.

ROLAND: Did you buy something, Tre?

CALLER: I bought lots! I got the Bayard Rustin T-shirt, the James Baldwin scotch decanter.

ROLAND: Great, Tre, and you should be proud to shop here because a portion of all sales goes to fight AIDS.

(They bow their heads solemnly)

CALLER: Really? How much?

JAMAL: Excuse me? What? I think we have a bad connection, Tre.

(The caller is disconnected)

TOGETHER: Bye, bye. Shop again.

JAMAL: Next item!

ROLAND: Many of you were in New York last June for the Gay Games and Stonewall 25.

JAMAL: Stonewall.

ROLAND: Stonewall.

TOGETHER: STONEWALL!

JAMAL: Where Black and Puerto Rican drag queens stood up for our rights. *(They stand)* Then they sat down. *(They sit)*

ROLAND: And had a little cocktail. Well, what better way to commemorate those drag queens than to dress like one. Item number Q-25. We call it the Fierce Black Drag Queen Kit.

JAMAL: Modeled here by the lovely Taekwanda.

(Taekwanda, a low "ho," enters and sashays across the stage)

TOGETHER: Hey, Taekwanda!

TAEKWANDA: Hey!

ROLAND: Taekwanda is here with us today on a work-release program.

TAEKWANDA: Hey!

ROLAND: The Fierce Black Drag Queen Kit is available in all sizes from miss junior petite thing to grand diva XL. Please specify shoe size, butt size, breast size, and wig size.

JAMAL: Taekwanda is featuring the leopard print sarong top.

(She models)

ROLAND: Very sixties retro, kind of Tamara Dobson as Cleopatra Jones, kind of . . .

ALL: Freeze sucka! Freeze sucka!

JAMAL: And underneath it reveals a stunning blue sequin mini.

(Taekwanda throws open the sarong with a hip swivel)

TAEKWANDA: Bam!

ROLAND: Very nice!

JAMAL: And that wig.

ROLAND: As Ntozake Shange would say, in the style of "a simple Black bitch with a bad attitude." Order now and we'll throw in the one item no fierce Black drag queen, like Taekwanda, would be caught dead at a riot without.

JAMAL: An authentic June 1969 Stonewall brick!

(Taekwanda pulls a brick out of her purse)

TAEKWANDA: Sylvester died for your sins!

(Taekwanda rants and raves)

ROLAND: Oh my! We're going to take a little break here and adjust Taekwanda's medication, but stay with us, next hour: Red Ribbon Pins . . .

JAMAL: In "diamondnesse"!

TAEKWANDA: Harvey Milk lives!

JAMAL: Right here on QVC!

TOGETHER: The Queer Value Channel.

TAEKWANDA: I have one thing to say! My name's not Taekwanda!

ROLAND and JAMAL: No!

(Tape of Nina Simone's "Four Women" plays as Taekwanda lip-synchs the last phrase)

TAPE: My name is *Peaches!*

(Taekwanda strikes a rebellious pose as lights drop to silhouette)

(Blackout)

Towards a Black
Queer Rhythm Nation

by Brian Freeman

(Whitesnake's "Bad Boys" plays as a young Black gay enters dressed in the style of the Queer Nation kids: leather jacket, white T-shirt, babushka on his head, chains around his neck. He dances like a nerdy rocker and sings along, strumming an air guitar)

KID: *(singing)* "I'm the black sheep in my family!" *(He cuts the music off)* Whitesnake. Cool, huh? They're racist. Sexist. If you could actually decode the lyrics, they're probably homophobic, but they are so cool! Do you think if you're Black and you're queer and a bit of a metalhead, that's a truly transgressive act? Huh? Huh, I'm trying to be a rebel, but I'm having trouble finding a cause. I used to hang out with the Lesbian/Gay/Bisexual/Transgender/Queer Student Alliance. There aren't actually any transgender persons in the Lesbian/Gay/Bisexual/Transgender/Queer Student Alliance, but if one shows up, they're covered! The kids in the Alliance, they swear they are the last transgressives, but you know what? They bother me, they really bother me.

Last meeting, we're having a discourse on the efficacy of staging a direct action at Toys "Я" Us. We break into subgroups, and start dialoguing our way through our various isms and schisms, and the facilitator comes in with his four different colored Magic Markers and big pieces of paper and we write down all our issues and tape them up to the wall and this is going on for hours, as you might imagine, and I'm thinking if some little six-year-old future homophobe wants to buy a Mr. Potato Head, let him. I finally stand up and say, "Yo, dudes. Dykes. I mean, dykes, dudes. I am beginning to feel oppressed by all this clonedom here. I don't want to put stickers on the back of my leather jacket, that reminds me of my parents' Volvo!" Then Joey, this white dude from my Foucault seminar, thinks he is so hip, says, "Oppressed? Your parents make more dough than the Huxtables. When they found out you were gay, they threw a coming-out party. You've never felt oppression in your life." I say, "Yo, dude. You know what you can do? Deconstruct this *(He flips the finger)*, dude!" Then Aurora, this face-ring lesbian, you know. *(He indicates various points of piercing)* Aurora jumps in: "As a woman, w-o-m-y-n, who continually struggles with the white male hegemony of this organization, I am in solidarity with the oppression felt by my Black gay brother . . ." And I'm, like, Aurora, spare me your seventies sense of self-righteousness! I can get that at home!

I split. I head for The Stud. I just want a drink and forget this whole thing. Guess what? Old clone night. Everyone is over twenty-two. Nothing but muscle bunnies in the joint. *(He flexes)* All pumping away to that dun-dun music. You know, DUN DUN DUN DA DA DA DUN DUN. *(He dances in seventies disco style)* Please! Talk about oppressive! But I don't care. I go over to the bar and start drowning my sorrows in sodium-free mineral water, when I hear this sound!

(Two actors sing the melody from "We Are" [Pomo Afro Homo's signature music] on-mike from offstage)

I think, "Whoa! Is there benzine in all mineral water now?" I order a beer, but two sips and I hear it again.

(Actors sing another phrase of the melody)

This is seriously freaking what little cool I have left. I look around the club to see if anyone else is hearing this, but everyone is still pumping away. DUN DUN DUN DA DA DA DUN DUN. Everyone except the one other Black person there. *(Actor enters dressed like an urban dance hall diva)* We'd seen each other before but never spoke.

DIVA: You had a lot of attitude. I thought you were tired.

KID: You had a lot of attitude. But we look at each other, and . . . *(To audience) (Kid and Diva sing the melody)* Like close encounters of the third kind! And he says . . .

DIVA: This club is tired. Let's get out of here.

KID: So we split for The Box, this funk and soul, no rock 'n' roll club, and on the way I tell him what happened at the meeting and he says . . .

DIVA: Those white kids are real tired.

KID: And I think that's a rather simplistic analysis of what is actually a complex sociological construction. But then, I'd never thought of it that way before. I thought, you know, we're all queer, so we're all . . . you know.

DIVA: Right.

KID: Well, we get to The Box.

DIVA: It had snowed in there too. Won't they leave us nothing? It was tired, with three *i*'s.

KID: The crowd *was* kinda monochromatic. But the DJ was playing rap, hip-hop, industrial, techno . . .

DIVA: That white girl is seriously tired.

KID: But I'm having a mood swing for the better, and we start to dance. But before we can even break a sweat, it happens again.

(An actor sings the melody on-mike from offstage)

The two of us look around and see this brother coming toward us like Nanook of the North fighting his way through a blizzard in one of those retro Hollywood movies. He pops out of the crowd and says . . .

STREET KID: Ooh, ooh, my ass! I'm here to dance. Let's kick it!

(CeCe Peniston's "We Got A Love Thang" blasts the silence. They all dance)

KID: *(Over music)* Kick it? We blasted off! It was like the starship *Enterprise* had particle-beamed us into another reality.

DIVA: I looked up at the DJ booth, and Sylvester had moved that white girl out the way. He said, "Honey, that's cute, but let's get real!"

STREET KID: Willi Smith and Patrick Kelly were fluttering up above in the fiercest drag I'd ever seen. I want that suit, Willi, I want that suit.

KID: And James Baldwin was behind the bar, pouring free drinks for himself and everybody else. He pops me open a sodium-free mineral water. I tell him about what happened at the Les/Gay/Bi/Trans/Queer Student Alliance meeting, and about my real fear, that maybe what Joey said is true. That maybe I am just a spoiled suburban brat with nothing more than an arm-chair understanding of oppression. James says *(becoming James Baldwin):* "My dear young boy. *You* are a Black queer growing up in America. I think you've hit the jackpot! Work it, my dear. Work it!"

(They all dance. The music fades out)

KID: At two A.M. they put us and all our dark diva delusions out of there.

STREET KID: But we were still wired.

DIVA: Not the least bit tired.

KID: So we decided to commit a truly, truly transgressive act. You know what we did? We went back to my place, made a pot of decaf, and just—talked. Cool, huh?

(Blackout)

A playwright, performance artist, radio personality, housecleaner, chain-smoker, and erstwhile Macy's elf, **david sedaris** lives in New York City. His work has been featured in *Harper's,* and he has been profiled in the *New York Times*. His collection of stories and essays, *Barrel Fever,* was published by Little, Brown in 1994.

david sedaris

Glen's Homophobia Newsletter, Vol. 3, No. 2

DEAR Subscriber,

First of all, I'd like to apologize for the lack of both the spring and summer issues of *Glen's Homophobia Newsletter*. I understand that you subscribed with the promise that this was to be a quarterly publication—four seasons' worth of news from the front lines of our constant battle against oppression. That was my plan. It's just that last spring and summer were so overwhelming that I, Glen, just couldn't deal with it all.

I'm hoping you'll understand. Please accept as consolation the fact that this issue is almost twice as long as the others. Keep in mind the fact that it's not easy to work forty hours a week *and* produce a quarterly publication. Also, while I'm at it, I'd like to mention that it would be wonderful if everyone who *read Glen's Homophobia Newsletter* also *subscribed* to *Glen's Homophobia Newsletter*. It seems that many of you are very generous when it comes to lending issues to your friends and family. That is all well and good, as everyone should understand the passion with which we as a people are hated beyond belief.

But at the same time, it *costs* to put out a newsletter and every dollar helps. It costs to gather data, to Xerox, to staple and mail, let alone the cost of my personal time and energies. So if you don't mind, I'd rather you mention *Glen's Homophobia Newsletter* to everyone you know but tell them they'll have to subscribe for themselves if they want the whole story. Thank you for understanding.

As I stated earlier, last spring and summer were very difficult for me. In late April Steve Dolger and I broke up and went our separate ways. Steve Dolger (see newsletters volume 2, nos. 1–4, and volume 3, no. 1) turned out to be the most *homophobic* homosexual I've ever had the displeasure of knowing. He lives in constant fear; afraid to make any kind of mature emotional commitment, afraid of growing old and losing what's left of his hair, and afraid to file his state and federal income taxes (which he has not done since 1987). Someday, perhaps someday very soon, Steve Dolger's past will come back to haunt him. We'll see how Steve and his little seventeen-year-old boyfriend feel when it happens!

Steve was very devious and cold during our breakup. I felt the chill of him well through the spring and late months of summer. With deep feelings come deep consequences, and I, Glen, spent the last two seasons of my life in what I can only describe as a waking coma—blind to the world around me, deaf to the cries of suffering others, mutely unable to express the stirrings of my wildly shifting emotions.

I just came out of it last Thursday.

What has Glen discovered? I have discovered that living blind to the world around you has its drawbacks but, strangely, it also has its rewards. While I was cut off from the joys of, say, good food and laughter, I was also blind to the overwhelming *homophobia* that is our everlasting cross to bear.

I thought that for this edition of the newsletter I might write something along the lines of a *homophobia* "Week in Review" but this single week has been much too much for me. Rather, I will recount a single day.

My day of victimization began at 7:15 A.M. when I held the telephone receiver to my ear and heard Drew Pierson's voice shouting "Fag, Fag, Fag" over and over and over again. It rings in my ears still. "Fag! I'll kick your ass good and hard the next time I see you. Goddamn you, Fag!" You, reader, are probably asking yourself, "Who is this Drew Pierson and why is he being so *homophobic* toward Glen?"

It all began last Thursday. I stopped into Dave's Kwik Stop on my way home from work and couldn't help but notice the cashier, a bulky, shorthaired boy who had "athletic scholarship" written all over his broad, dullish face and DREW PIERSON: I'M HERE TO HELP! printed on a name tag pinned to his massive chest. I took a handbasket and bought, I believe, a bag of charcoal briquettes and a quartered fryer. At the register this Drew fellow rang up the items and said, "I'll bet you're going home to grill you some chicken."

I admitted that it was indeed my plan. Drew struck me as being very perceptive and friendly. Most of the Kwik Stop employees are *homophobic,* but something about Drew's manner led me to believe that he was different, sensitive, and open. That evening, sitting on my patio and staring into the glowing embers nestled in my tiny grill, I thought of Drew Pierson and for the first time in months I felt something akin to a beacon of hope flashing through the darkness of my mind. I, Glen, smiled.

I returned to Dave's Kwik Stop the next evening and bought some luncheon meat, a loaf of bread, potato chips, and a roll of toilet paper.

At the cash register Drew rang up my items and said, "I'll bet you're going on a picnic in the woods!"

The next evening I had plans to eat dinner at the condominium of my sister and her *homophobic* husband, Vince Covington (see newsletter volume 1, no. 1). On the way to their home I stopped at the Kwik Stop, where I bought a can of snuff. I don't use snuff, wouldn't think of it. I only ordered snuff because it was one of the few items behind the counter and on a lower shelf. Drew, as an employee, is forced to wear an awkward garment—sort of a cross between a vest and a sandwich board. The terrible synthetic thing ties at the sides and falls practically to the middle of his thighs. I only ordered the snuff so that as he bent over to fetch it, I might get a more enlightened view of Drew's physique. Regular readers of this newsletter will understand what I am talking about. Drew bent over and squatted on his heels, saying, "Which one? Tuberose? I used to like me some snuff. I'll bet you're going home to relax with some snuff, aren't you?"

The next evening, when I returned for more snuff, Drew explained that he was a freshman student at Carteret County Community College, where he majors in psychology. I was touched by his naïveté. CCCC might as well print their diplomas on tar paper. One would take a course in diesel mechanics or pipe fitting, but under no circumstances should one study

psychology at CCCC. That is where certified universities recruit their studies for *abnormal* psychology. CCCC is where the
missing links brood and stumble and swing from the outer
branches of our educational system.

Drew, bent over, said that he was currently taking a course
in dreams. The teacher demands that each student keep a note-
book, but Drew, exhausted after work, sleeps, he said, "like a
gin-soaked log," and wakes remembering nothing.

I told him I've had some interesting dreams lately, because
it's true, I have.

Drew said, "Symbolic dreams? Dreams that you could turn
around when you're awake and make sense of?"

I said, yes, haunting dreams, meaningful, dense.

He asked then, hunkered down before the snuff, if I would
relate my dreams to him. I answered, yes indeed, and he slapped
a tin of snuff on the counter and said, "On the house!"

I returned home, my heart a bright balloon. Drew may be
young, certainly—perhaps no older than, say, Steve Dolger's
current boyfriend. He may not be able to hold his own during
strenuous intellectual debate, but neither can most people. My
buoyant spirit carried me home, where it was immediately de-
flated by the painful reminder that my evening meal was to
consist of an ethnic lasagna pathetically submitted earlier that
day by Melinda Delvecchio, a lingering temp haunting the sec-
retarial pool over at the office in which I work. Melinda, stout,
inquisitive, and bearded as a potbellied pig, has taken quite a
shine to me. She is clearly and mistakenly in love with me and
presents me, several times a week, with hideous dishes pro-
tected with foil. "Someone needs to fatten you up," she says,
placing her eager hooves against my stomach. One would think

that Melinda Delvecchio's kindness might come as a relief to the grinding *homophobia* I encounter at the office.

One might think that Melinda Delvecchio is thoughtful and generous until they pull back the gleaming foil under which lies her hateful concoction of overcooked pasta stuffed with the synthetic downy fluff used to fill plush toys and cheap cushions. Melinda Delvecchio is no friend of mine—far from it —and, regarding the heated "lasagna" steaming before me, I made a mental note to have her fired as soon as possible.

That night I dreamt that I was forced to leave my home and move underground into a dark, subterranean chamber with low, muddy ceilings and no furniture. That was bad enough, but to make matters worse, I did not live alone but had to share the place with a community of honest-to-God trolls. These were small trolls with full beards and pointy, curled shoes. The trolls were hideously and relentlessly merry. They called me by name, saying, "Glen, so glad you could join us! Look, every-body, Glen's here! Welcome aboard, friend!" They were all so agreeable and satisfied with my company that I woke up sweating at 6 A.M. and could not return to sleep for fear of them.

I showered twice and shaved my face, passing the time until seven, at which point I phoned Drew at his parents' home. He answered groggy and confused. I identified myself and paused while he went to fetch a pencil and tablet with which to record my story.

Regular readers of *Glen's Homophobia Newsletter* know that I, Glen, honor truth and hold it above all other things. The truth, be it ugly or naked, does not frighten me. The meaner the truth, the harder I, Glen, stare it down. However, on this occasion I decided to make an exception. My dreaming of trolls means absolutely nothing. It's something that came to me in my sleep and is of no real importance. It is our waking dreams, our daydreams, that are illuminating. Regular readers of *Glen's Homophobia Newsletter* know that I dream of the day when our people can walk the face of this earth free of the terrible *homophobia* that binds us. What are sleeping dreams but so much garbage? I can't bear to hear other people's dreams unless I myself am in them.

I put all these ideas together in a manageable sort of way and told Drew Pierson that I dreamt I was walking through a forest of angry, vindictive trees.

"Like those hateful trees in *The Wizard of Oz*?" he said. "Those mean trees that threw the apples?"

"Yes," I said, "exactly."

"Did any of them hit you?" he asked, concerned.

"A few."

"Ouch! Then what?"

I told him I came upon a clearing where I saw a single tree, younger than the rest but stocky, a husky, good-looking tree that spoke to me, saying, "I'll bet you're tired of being hated, aren't you?"

I could hear Drew scratching away with his pencil and repeating my dictation: "I . . . bet . . . you're . . . tired . . . of . . . being . . . hated . . ."

I told Drew that the tree had spoken in a voice exactly like his own, low and firm, yet open and friendly.

"Like my voice, really?" He seemed pleased. "Damn, my voice on a tree. I never thought about a thing like that."

That night I dreamt I was nailed to a cross that was decorated here and there with fragrant tulips. I glanced over at the cross next to me, expecting to see Christ, but instead, nailed there, I saw Don Rickles. We waved to each other and he mouthed the words "Hang in there."

I called Drew the next morning and told him I once again dreamt I was in a forest clearing. Once again I found myself face-to-face with a husky tree.

Drew asked, "What did the tree say this time?"

I told him the tree said, "Let me out! Let me out! I'm yearning to break free."

"Break free of what?" he asked.

"Chains and limitations," I said. "The tree said, 'Strip me of my bark, strip me of my bark.' "

"The tree said that to you personally or was there someone else standing around?"

I told him the tree spoke to me personally and that I had no choice but to do as I was told. I peeled away the bark with my bare hands and out stepped Drew, naked and unashamed.

"Naked in the woods? I was in the woods naked like that? Then what?"

I told Drew I couldn't quite remember what happened next; it was right on the tip of my mind where I couldn't quite grasp it.

Drew said, "I want to know what I was doing naked in the woods is what I want to know."

I said, "Are you naked now?"

"Now?" Drew, apparently uncertain, took a moment before saying, "No. I got my underwear on."

I suggested that if he put the telephone receiver into the pouch of his briefs, it might trigger something that would help me recall the rest of my dream.

I heard the phone muffle. When I yelled "Did you put the phone where I told you to?" I heard a tiny, far-off voice say, "Yes, I sure did. It's there now."

"Jump up and down," I yelled. "Jump."

I heard shifting sounds as Drew's end of the telephone jounced around in his briefs. I heard him yell, "Are you re-membering yet?" And then, in the distance, I heard a woman's voice screaming, "Drew Pierson, what in the name of God are you doing with that telephone? Other people have to put their mouth on that thing too, you know. You should be strung up for doing a thing like that, goddamn you." I heard Drew say that he was doing it in order to help someone remember a dream. Then I heard the words "moron," "shit for brains," and the inevitable "fag." As in "Some fag put you up to this, didn't he? Goddamn you."

Then Drew must have taken the receiver out of his briefs because suddenly I could hear him loud and clear and what I heard was *homophobia* at its worst. "Fag! Fag! I'll kick your ass good and hard the next time I see you. Goddamn you to hell." The words still echo in my mind.

I urge all my readers to BOYCOTT DAVE'S KWIK STOP. I urge you to phone Drew Pierson anytime day or night and tell him you dreamt you were sitting on his face. Drew Pierson's home (ophobic) telephone number is 555-5008. Call him and raise your voice against *homophobia!*

So that, in a nutshell, was my morning. I pulled myself together and subjected myself to the daily *homophobia* conven-tion that passes as my job. Once there, I was scolded by my devious and *homophobic* department head for accidentally shred-ding some sort of disputed contract. Later that afternoon I was confronted, once again, by that casserole-wielding mastodon, Melinda Delvecchio, who grew tearful when informed that I would sooner dine on carpet remnants than another of her foil-covered ethnic slurs.

On my way home from the office I made the mistake of stopping at the Food Carnival, where I had no choice but to park in one of the so-called "handicapped" spaces. Once inside the store I had a tiff with the *homophobic* butcher over the dictionary definition of the word "cutlet." I was completely ignored by the *homophobic* chimpanzee they've hired to run the produce department, and I don't even want to talk about the cashier. After collecting my groceries I returned to the parking lot, where I encountered a *homophobe* in a wheelchair, relentlessly bashing my car again and again with the foot pedals of his little chariot. Regular readers of *Glen's Homophobia Newsletter* know that I, Glen, am not a violent man. Far from it. But in this case I had no choice but to make an exception. My daily *homophobia* quota had been exceeded and I, Glen, struck back with brute physical force.

Did it look good? No, it did not.

But I urge you, reader, to understand. Understand my position as it is your own.

Understand and subscribe, subscribe.

bob smith started doing stand-up in Buffalo, New York, before moving to New York City, where he performed openly gay material in clubs like The Comic Strip, Catch a Rising Star, and The Improvisation.

In 1989 Bob joined forces with Jaffe Cohen and Danny McWilliams to create Funny Gay Males, whose initial two-week engagement at The Duplex in Greenwich Village turned into an award-winning two-year run. They have performed for sold-out houses in major venues across the country and had the honor of performing at the 1993 March on Washington for an audience of one million people. Cohen, McWilliams and Smith have written a book, *Growing Up Gay,* to be published by Hyperion Books (owned by Walt Disney!) in 1995.

Smith's many television appearances include *The Joan Rivers Show, Evening at the Improv, Tom Snyder,* and he covered The Gay Games for *Howard Stern.* Smith was also a performer and head writer for Comedy Central's *Out There* and was hired to write the monologues for a screenplay about a gay stand-up comic for Steven Spielberg's company, Amblin. Bob has the distinction of having been the first gay stand-up comic to appear on *The Tonight Show with Jay Leno* and in his own HBO comedy half hour.

bob smith

The Gay Agenda

It wasn't easy telling my family that I'm gay. I made my carefully worded announcement at Thanksgiving. It was very Norman Rockwell. I said, "Mom, would you please pass the gravy to a homosexual?"

She passed it to my father. A terrible scene followed. Just kidding, Dad.

Then, my Aunt Lorraine said, "Bob, you're gay? Are you seeing a psychiatrist?"

I said, "No, I'm seeing a lieutenant in the Navy."

We talk about everything in my family now. I remember last year we were talking about gay marriages and my brother Greg said, "Bob, you're gay—what do you think?" And my mother said, "Greg, that's not nice. Don't remind him." Oh yeah, Mom. That had entirely slipped my mind.

At first my parents didn't know what to tell their friends. They'd introduce me by saying, "This is Bob, our youngest son. He's thirty-three years old, unmarried, and it's none of your business."

Now Mom's reached the point in her life where she doesn't care what people think. She has a bumper sticker on her car that says HONK, IF YOUR HUSBAND'S WATCHING TV AND YOUR OLDEST SON DOESN'T KNOW WHAT HE'S DOING, THE OTHER TWO ARE IN CALIFORNIA AND NEW YORK, ONE'S GAY, YOUR DAUGHTER'S DIVORCED, AND YOU FORGOT TO BUY MILK WHILE AT THE STORE.

I was just in Buffalo, where I grew up. We had a Dysfunctional Family Reunion. You've all been to them, right? Where everyone has to bring a casserole and an unresolved issue. I brought Tuna Surprise and my boyfriend Tom. Both were *big* hits.

I saw my favorite relative, my Aunt Lorraine. My friends love her. When she came to visit me in New York, I picked her up at the airport and we had to take the George Washington Bridge because her hair wouldn't fit through the Lincoln Tunnel.

Aunt Lorraine's a chain-smoker. She's always lighting another cigarette. True story. She once saved a man's life by giving him mouth-to-mouth resuscitation—six months later he was dead from emphysema.

While in Buffalo, my parents took me out to dinner—at a $6.99 all-you-can-eat cafeteria. They had a salad made with lime jello with celery and peas in it.

Straight people, here's a little tip: Don't combine foods by color. If it was a good idea, a gay man would've done it years ago.

The first gay bar I ever went to was in Buffalo and I remember walking in the door and I couldn't see anything because they had a fog machine on the dance floor. I thought, "Great. The last thing we need in Buffalo is bad weather indoors too."

I'm very close to my family, and when I was in California, I visited my sister. We took my niece to the zoo, and at one point she said, "Uncle Bob, when are you going to get married?" And I said, "Amanda, I'm gay. Do you know what that means?"

And she said, "I think so. Are you a top or a bottom?"

She's growing up a little too fast.

A lot of people are upset about gay parents. In South Carolina a state representative wants to outlaw gay men and lesbians from adopting children because he believes gay households are "breeding grounds for future homosexuals."

I'm only going to explain this once: *Heterosexuals* are the breeding grounds for future homosexuals. I know it's hard to believe.

The idea that your parents influence your sexual orientation is ridiculous. Because if it were true, I'd have my mother's taste in men, and I've never dated a guy who falls asleep in his chair during *Jeopardy!*

Well, having two gay dads *would* have its advantages. You know you'd always have the best Halloween costume on the block.

Does this sound like I'm promoting homosexuality? I hate that phrase, "promoting homosexuality." I've never received any of

the promotional literature. All right, one *International Male* cata-
log . . .

We're everywhere. We're even in the Mafia. Don't mess
with the Gay Mafia—they'll break the legs on your coffee
table. You could end up in the river wearing cement
pumps.

I was in Los Angeles during the riots, and it's a little-
known fact but there were gay looters. They all got caught.
They'd spent five hours in stores trying things on.

I did a show in Kentucky and guess what? There is Gay
White Trash. They're easy to spot. In front of their trailer,
there's a broken Cuisinart on cinder blocks.

Now I know homophobia is based on ignorance, but I hate
the really stupid questions. Someone once asked me, "What's
this thing gay people have with Judy Garland?"

I said, "I don't know. What's this thing that straight people
have with Elvis?"

Listen, I don't care whether you're gay or straight—if
you're obsessed with a dead celebrity, you're a loser.

Now you know I'm gay and you know I'm from Buffalo, but I
feel the most important fact you should know about me, something that influenced my entire outlook on life, is that my
birthday's on December 24.

And from years of experience, we people with December
birthdays now know what the Three Wise Men said when they
delivered their gifts: "These are for both your birthday and
Christmas." The cheap fucks.

According to the Bible, the Three Wise Men didn't even

deliver their gifts until January 6. Being wise, they shopped after Christmas.

Last year, for my birthday (and Christmas), I was given a puppy. It's half poodle and half pit bull. It's not a good attack dog but it's a vicious gossip.

My brother-in-law's Jewish and he and my sister celebrate both holiday traditions. At Christmas they set up a Nativity scene but all the figures look skeptical.

My parents keep their Nativity scene up until Easter, when it ascends to the attic.

At Christmas my friend Kevin sets up the most elaborate Nativity scene that I've ever encountered. He thinks it's Barbie's Dream House. He's made Mary over forty-five different outfits. I don't think she needs a little black cocktail dress.

One year he did this *Wizard of Oz* theme—there were two little feet sticking out from under the manger. He's out of his mind.

Now, Kevin's an unbelievable queen. He's a partner in a gay law firm: Baubles, Bangles and Beads. The air bag in his car is a clutch. At his gym he uses the spiral StairMaster—to make a dramatic entrance.

Every year my lesbian friends Sharon and Patty set up a Nativity scene. They call it the Birthing Center. They think it's great that Mary practiced supernatural childbirth and didn't have the baby in a hospital and, better yet, that she had a baby without touching a man.

I was raised Roman Catholic and the Catholic Church is against homosexuality. It seems hypocritical—one of the priests at our parish was gay. Father Mary Louise. He always tried to make you feel comfortable at confession:

"*Then* what happened?

"You're kidding.

"Stop.

"Wait a minute, before you go on—I'm going to get a drink. You want one?

"Well, then, go in peace. Your sins, some of which are remarkable, are forgiven. And for your penance, watch *The Ten Commandments* three times. Wasn't Anne Baxter terrible?"

I have a little confession to make. In college I experimented with heterosexuality. I slept with a straight guy. I was really drunk.

My best friend in college, Ted, was straight and I remember when Ted and I would go to fraternity parties where Ted would meet a woman and start to undress her with his eyes while I'd be putting her in a whole new outfit.

When Ted got married, I was his best man and I was responsible for his bachelor party. It was fine but everyone hated my stag movie, Hayley Mills in *The Trouble with Angels*. I love that movie.

I've been in a relationship for five years with a guy named Tom, an actor. Tom went to a Catholic high school for the performing arts, Our Lady Sings Sondheim. It was fabulous. Everyone's yearbook photo was eight-by-ten.

Tom and I are becoming more militant. We want the same rights as straight couples to hold hands and make a public display of affection, even if we do avoid intimacy in the privacy of our own home.

After almost six years, our relationship is a little less romantic. I recently said, "Tom, I have a swimmer's build."

He said, "Yeah, so do flounder."

Tom doesn't like it when I notice other guys. He knows my type—gay men who really assert their masculinity. Muscles, tattoos, Ethel Merman impersonators.

Tom complains that I don't do any housework. Hey, I was up-front about that. I'm lazy. My hero's Rip van Winkle. Now the story is that he slept for twenty years. That's not true. He slept eight hours, but for twenty years lay in bed for a few more minutes.

I recently discovered an amazing statistic. It said that nine out of ten lesbian couples and six out of ten gay couples now have some form of marriage or commitment ceremony. I should've known this because last year my friends Patty and Sharon had a commitment ceremony but I thought the invitation was a little too politically correct:

> Sharon Bartlett and Patty Marks want to invite you on this piece of recycled paper to their handicapped-accessible, signed-for-the-hearing-impaired commitment ceremony in an Indian sweat lodge on April 19th.
>
> A joyous lactose-intolerant, sugar-free, vegetarian, in-recovery reception will immediately follow.
>
> The wedding cake will be made out of lentils for those allergic to wheat.

I love them dearly but I keep telling them there's a fine line between holistic and assholistic. People need to remember that.

Last year newspapers in Kansas and Minnesota started printing gay and lesbian wedding announcements. This is great news. I can't wait until every newspaper in America starts doing this:

> Mr. and Mrs. Stephen Douglas have reluctantly announced the engagement of their son Timothy to Mark Feldman, the son of the stunned Dr. and Mrs. Saul Feldman. A May commitment ceremony is planned, with an awkward reception to immediately follow.
>
> At the parents' request, there will be an open bar during the ceremony.

Well, Tom and I have never had a commitment ceremony but we did buy commitment rings in Provincetown. It seems like another big trend this year is having your body pierced.

Come on, there are times when a fashion statement is a cry for help. I saw this guy who had four rings through his ear, four rings through his eyebrow, four through his nose. At what point do you hang a shower curtain?

I hate trendy stuff. Sharon did a weekend workshop where she walked barefoot over hot coals to prove that she could do anything. So now Sharon keeps telling me, "Bob, you create your own reality."

No, Sharon. *Psychotics* create their own reality. That's an important distinction. Let's not lose that.

The Gay and Lesbian Agenda

I became really angry when I learned that right-wing groups in this country have been sending out a video called "The Gay Agenda," which claims to represent our community. It's all lies. But I do think the idea of a gay and lesbian agenda is great, so I've come up with a preliminary one. I think you can boil it down to two items:

1. Full civil rights. This includes gays in the military, gay marriages, gay couples at high school proms, national health insurance, AIDS research and education, and anything else we can think of that will terrify Pat Robertson.
2. We want our national anthem to have a twenty-five-minute dance version.

I think that's very reasonable.

In 1990 **SUZANNE WESTENHOEFER** burst onto the comedy scene, winning a contest at Kelly's Piano Bar in New York. As an out lesbian onstage, Suzanne performs for every type of audience, playing major comedy clubs and concert halls throughout the United States. In July 1994, in her own HBO half-hour comedy special, Suzanne stepped into the living rooms of this country with the same out lesbian comedy that has challenged stereotypes and broken down barriers from Texas to Oregon and from New York to Florida.

Besides her own HBO special, Suzanne has had major television exposure on ABC's *Day One,* A&E's *An Evening at the Improv,* VH-1's *Buster's Comedy Hour, Caroline's Comedy Hour* and *Out There* on Comedy Central, and a host of other network and cable appearances. Recently she won New York City's Outstanding Achievement Award for Comedy, and her nationwide tour is receiving spectacular reviews around the country.

suzanne westenhoefer

Nothing in My Closet but My Clothes

Hello, I'm Suzanne Westenhoefer, famous lesbian comedian. Like you know so many who say they're lesbians. Only kidding. What I do is gay comedy in straight clubs across the country. Kind of my version of S-M. Quite frankly, it's a little scary. In New York, I play places like Catch a Rising Star and Caroline's, but there is this one club . . . Three times I auditioned for them and three times I did really well, but that little worm of a manager came up to me and said, "Oh, you're really good, but I don't think we can use you, 'cause we groom our people for TV, and I don't think there'll ever be LESBIANS on TV." And I'm like, no lesbians on TV? What about Wimbledon? How about Alice on *The Brady Bunch*? Oh, and I guess you didn't know about Miss Jane Hathaway on *The Beverly Hillbillies*. She was a big dyke. Didn't you think so? I totally identified with her when I was twelve years old. I thought it was because I wanted to be a secretary . . . That wasn't it.

It's amazing now, isn't it? There are lots of lesbians on TV. How about on *Roseanne*? Yeah, Darlene, she's coming out any minute. Watching her is too much. It's like watching that little Buddy on *Family*. You know, it's like, STOP, my God. And then they bring the boyfriend in, and we're all going, "Yeah, right." Well, they had Jethro for Miss Jane . . . It ain't working. They had the butcher for Alice, but who was butcher than Alice?

This is really a fun time to be a lesbian . . . for a change. I mean everyone is coming out. Melissa Etheridge came out. Go, girl. k.d. lang came out. I love that. And then at the March on Washington, Martina Navratilova came out. Yeah, do you think there were about six people in Nebraska going: "Uhhhh, NO way. I would never have suspected her!" I love Martina. Do you love her? Don't you just want to lick that vein that sticks out on her arm? Oh, sorry, that's probably more information than you needed. You know, the coolest thing about Martina is through all the years she was Number One, and they were saying everything about her—she's a lesbian/she's bi/she's on steroids. She'd just go *(serves overhand)*, "Yeah, just give me another million dollars." I respect that. I thought it was pretty cool. I've been stalking this woman for eleven years, and the night before the March, I crashed a party and I MET her. I met Martina. I was so excited . . . but I was a total asshole. I thought I was going to be so cool. I got up to her, and I was, like . . . youknowithoughtwhen #$&*()$$$#*$ . . . TENNIS. And she goes, "Oh, I know you, you're that lesbian comedian." And I'm freakin'. She looks at me and says, "I know you, 'cause you do jokes about me." I'm thinking, "Oh shit, which ones?" Then she goes . . . *(sticks out arm and* *shows vein)* No, I didn't lick it. I know, I'm kicking myself now, but I passed out. When I woke up, Cindy Crawford was shaving me . . . what the hell was that?

I've been traveling so much. I was down in Dallas, Texas, doing lesbian comedy at a straight club . . . Shoot me in the head. What was I thinking? It actually went very well. In five weeks I was never heckled once. 'Course I told 'em if they heckled me, they'd have gay kids. There was one man, though, who had a sort of "moment," and he felt the need to share it with me during my show. He looked at me and said, "Hey, did you get that way because you had some kind of bad sexual experience with a guy?" I'm like, "Yeah—like, if that's all it took, the entire female population would be gay, sir, and I'd be here talking about the weather, all right?"

You know what I've found out while I've been traveling? It's the most amazing thing. Straight people are afraid of us. Don't you love it? It's true. I mean, I had a woman totally flip out on me when she found out I was a lesbian. "Oh, my God. Now that I know you're a lesbian, I can't get undressed in front of you." I'm like, "Really, miss, just take my order." Who are these McDonald's people? But I've always wondered, if they're afraid of us, how afraid of us *are* they? Do straight people get in little groups and go, "Oh, my God, Bill, don't go down there. That's a homosexual neighborhood." Oh, yeah, they'll do your hair. Haven't you heard about all those drive-by, gay perm-jackings? "Get out, you look like hell . . . *[combs and teases hair]* All right, you can go." Oh, we're fearsome. And they're afraid of us in the military. That's funny. You know, the thing that's so weird is, a couple of years ago, when I was bartending at a straight club, 'cause I'm liberal, there was this guy who would come on to me. He said, "Too bad, Suzanne, you're a homosexual, so you can't serve in the military." Ohhhh, big deal. How will I live with the disappointment? It's like, HELLO, I didn't want to go. Like I want to get up that early? I don't think so. I would be the original Private Benjamin, I would not be happy about it. What do they care if we're in *their* military? I've often thought anyway . . . if they don't want us, let's not go. All the gay people in the military, get out. 'Cause you know we'll go to war again. You know we will. And then that will mean that all the straight people have to go and fight and die for our rights, and we get to hang here. "Bye, you be careful . . . Hey, we'll take care of your wives." It's just all in the way you look at it.

Ever been up to Provincetown? That's fun. I was up there for ten weeks this year. But it's really weird, because you know what happened this year? There are straight people there. What the hell is that all about? What are they doing there? You know what else? Have you been to San Francisco? There are straight people there too. Are they not reading the literature correctly? "Excuse me, excuse me . . . straight person, you're in Key West . . . GET OUT!" I feel especially annoyed about it in Provincetown, because that is really the only gay mecca that's almost totally gay, right? So when straight people are there, I'm kinda like, "Excuse me, we have one tip of one tiny little state, and you have the whole REST OF THE FREAKIN'

UNITED STATES!" Of course, I say that in a very supportive, sisterly kind of way.

So I was in San Francisco and this friend of mine who is really young—she's twenty-one, you know, lesbian larva—she says, "I really want to take you to this place called Good Vibrations." I thought it was a dance club. But it's not. It's an erotic sex toy shop. Have you ever been to one of these places? What the hell is that shit? I've been in a ten-year relationship, I get out, and I find there are dildos shaped like woodchucks. Whose fantasy is that? "Oh, honey, put on the woodchuck, that gets me hot, yeah. Uuh, you know what, wear the gopher . . . I love the gopher." It's too weird. And I know you've seen that dildo shaped like a dolphin. Look, kids, I'm an animal lover like anybody, but if someone came at me with a dolphin strapped on 'em, I'd be like, "Honey, I don't know . . . suddenly I'm hungry for tuna." I want to know what you do with it anyway. Strap it on, go running into the bedroom: "Hi, honey, let's play Greenpeace. You be the big boat, then I'll try to sink you."

Some weird stuff going on out there. You know what I really don't understand? Why every time men watch a porno movie, there's always the obligatory lesbian sex scene. Do you know this? And, of course, you know they're using real lesbians . . . NOT. If you ever had the misfortune of seeing one of these things, they get it all wrong. They'll show two naked women lying on top of each other, holding hands, kissing, and simultaneously, they're both having orgasms. I'm like, is there someone here I can't see? Apparently, these directors think that all gay women do is rub against each other and then have an orgasm—which is not true, or there would be more of them on the dance floor.

There are a lot of places that gay people don't fit in . . . like Sears. Actually, the one that gets me the most is the bridal shower. *(Deep sigh)* Ah, there's a fun lesbian afternoon. What's a bridal shower if you are gay? Well, let me tell you, it's pretty much the parade of gifts you'll never get because you're a homosexual. It's like, "Come on in and take a look at the toaster, the blender, silverware you'll have to buy for yourself." I'll tell you right now, I don't bring a gift anymore, I take one. I've got six Cuisinarts now. I don't give a shit . . . they owe us. So, I'm at this bridal shower, and we play this game that is totally pertinent to my lifestyle. This woman gets up, and she's like, "OK, God . . . OK . . . I'm sure . . . OK . . . Are you ready? OK . . . The first question is this . . . Ah . . . OK . . . What could your husband do for you, like, on your wedding night, that would totally, truly satisfy you? *(giggle)*" So, I'm writing down stupid shit like "Oh, cut off his penis" or "Send in his sister." 'Cause, well, I didn't realize that we were going to have to read them out loud or that we didn't read our own, you know, but had to pass it to the person next to you. My mom is still really pissed.

Are you out to your parents? About three years ago, I was on *Sally Jesse Raphael,* and I came out to the nation, and I thought, "ummm . . . might want to tell my mom," 'cause I didn't want her channel-surfing one day (click, click, click): "Hey, isn't that my daughter? What the hell does that say under her name? . . . She's not Lebanese!"

So are you activists? Are you out in the community, doing active sort of stuff? ACT UP sort of stuff? Anyway, you know what's really funny about being an activist: you don't always agree, do you, about what you're for or against. Remember last year, *Basic Instinct* came out. All my friends were in my face going, "Oh, Suzanne, have you seen this movie, *Basic Instinct*? You have to hate it, because it really has a negative representation of lesbians in the movie. It seems that the lead character is a lesbian who seduces men into her apartment and then kills them with an ice pick." Yeah, so . . . is she dressed badly? Because like every time I see that stupid Andrew Dice Clay on television, I'm like, "Man, where the hell's *my* ice pick? Oh, I must've left it in Pat Buchanan." Hate him, hate his little girl-friend, Pat Robertson.

I go into high schools whenever I can and talk to the kids about what it's like to be gay. I let them ask all the questions they want to; then I just answer them. What I want to share with you are some of the actual questions the kids asked and the answers I would have given, had they not been sixteen. *(pulls out cards)* Do you love this, look, I laminated them. That's because I am anal-retentive. Oh, yeah, like none of you are. Maybe you don't know how to tell. Do you know how to tell? You're the anal-retentive one in the relationship if you sound like this a lot, when you're just standing around the apartment, *(sigh)* "Does that go there? Is that just going to pick itself up? Weren't these alphabetized when I left this morning?"

Anyway, READY? All right, first question. *Do you participate in foreplay?* No, I let her do all the work. You know, it's a really interesting thing: I always thought that I was this really aggressive butch top, 'cause, well, I was always on the top. Then I found out it's because I have asthma and I can't breathe on the bottom.

What are you thinking about when you are making love to another girl? That I'm taller, thinner, maybe a little more tanned, and she's Candice Bergen. Yes, I love her. Don't you? Remember when she first came out on those commercials: "Somebody ought to talk to you about how much time you're spending on the phone." YES! I got Sprint right away because I thought she was coming over. Never saw her.

Do you want to be a man? Only when I'm camping. That's a handy little gadget you guys have there, isn't it? 'Course you never get the thrill of squatting down in the middle of the forest in the middle of the night and going, "What's that? What's touching my butt? What is that? I don't have to go anymore." Isn't that the worst? Did you notice that no matter how far apart you get your legs, you could be doing some Mary Lou Retton thing, you know what I mean . . . you still pee in your damn sock. And it's so easy to tell where all the women are when you're camping, by the one sock hanging out to dry by each tent. Yes, I have been to music festivals. They camp there. I know, you're looking at me and thinking, "Hey, she looks like a pretty big camping babe." But you know, I would rather peel back my own skull and suck my brains out with a straw, than camp! Thank you. Camping is an evil, horrible thing. Kids, we built homes, let's live in them, OK?

My ex-girlfriend was a big camper. I don't mean she was an RV or anything, I mean she was a person who liked to camp. She bought one of those RVs, but I never wanted to go camping, so she used to trick me. Like, for example, I read these books on serial killers (it's just a thing), so it'd be like, Friday night in our apartment, and we'd be sitting around and I'd say, "Honey, where's my book on Ted Bundy?" "It's in the camper." "Well, how come it is in the camper? I don't remember it ever being . . ." "I don't know. Why don't you go out and look." So I'd go out to look, step up into the RV, and BOOM, the door would shut, I'm halfway to Maine. Have you ever been camping in an RV? It sucks. I hate it. What do you do for the first five hours, you're there? You back it into that square. That's all you do. So the entire first half of your vacation, you're going like this *(paces, giving hand signals to park the RV)* and then fight about it for an hour more, how you didn't do it right. It was so weird, too, because my girlfriend and I were such opposites. She was one of these microbiotic, health-healing, holistic, chiropractic, vegetarian kind of people. So we would go camping, and we'd be sitting around the fire, and I would have a martini, a hot dog, and a cigarette. I'm camping! Me and nature . . . party, party . . . *(sniff, sniff)* I smell dirt.

Where's my dustbuster? Look at this, there's dirt everywhere. I'll never get this place clean.

It was so funny, too, 'cause we would take the dogs, we had a golden retriever and a black Lab. Yeah, you know, goldens are great dogs, but, no offense—pretty dog, very stupid. I'm sorry, especially compared to the black Lab. But my black Lab is a wuss dog. Do you have wuss dogs? Do you know what I mean? Where they're like, these big, ugly, mean-looking dogs, but they're afraid of everything? And they don't want to get dirty? Wuss dogs are the ones where you go to let them out, and it's raining, and they go, "Oh, I can hold it . . . I'll just go behind the couch, later." My black Lab doesn't like to be dirty. It's hysterical. We'd go camping and the golden would go out and run in the dirt and be, "Ohhhh." And my black Lab would be, "God . . . shit." She'd hate it. Twenty-four hours into the trip, she'd be sitting behind the wheel, going, "Let's go . . . been here, done it . . . LET'S GO!"

Are you a lesbian by choice or by nature? Yes. That's the thing, that whole "choice" thing. People say, "Oh, you chose to be a homosexual." Oh no, I didn't choose it—I was chosen! Are you serious? I get to be queer? Oh, thank you. I didn't even fill out the application, I am sooo thrilled. No, I did. I bought the ticket, I scratched it off . . . Look, I'm a lesbian! I won!

Have you ever touched a man's penis? No, only a woman's. My mom hates that joke. She comes up to me after my show and says, "You do not have a penis, young lady. I bathed you. You are lying to all those people. They paid good money for you not to lie . . . they don't want to hear that stuff . . . You don't have a penis, do you?" You have to love my mom, she's so cool. She taped the whole March on Washington on C-SPAN, and she didn't watch it until I got home 'cause she wanted me to explain things to her. So for three hours I went like this with my mom: "Now, Mom, that's a woman . . . no, now that's a guy." It's true, RuPaul's up there, and my mom's freaking "NO WAY!"

How did you know you were gay . . . what did you feel? Apparently, another girl.

This is my favorite one. I have no joke for this. It is exactly what the child wrote. *When you have sex with a female, what do you put in your virginia?*

I'm in such a weird mood, don't know what it is. Maybe it's because I'm traveling. You know what? It's because I'm ovulating. Anybody else? Yeah, the egg is making the trip down the tube. I always feel so bad for my eggs, too, 'cause I'm a lesbian. Don't you? Don't you feel like your eggs are up there going, "Oh, big deal. Here we go again. We're never going to meet anybody."

"My Celibate Eggs," a poem by Suzanne Westenhoefer.

karen williams has played to standing-room-only audiences from coast to coast since 1984. Known as the Diva of Comedy, she has been the featured host on PBS's *In the Life,* a special guest on *Geraldo* for his "Lesbian Chic" segment, a performer during the 1993 March on Washington and Stonewall 25, and one of the stars for the second annual *Joan Rivers & Her Funny Friends,* benefiting the New York Lesbian and Gay Community Services Center. Olivia Records' cruises, women's music and comedy festivals, college campuses, and pride celebrations all serve as venues for Karen's unique comic appeal.

Williams is also a renowned writer, lecturer, workshop presenter, and human rights activist. She is a featured columnist for *Outlines,* a gay and lesbian Chicago-based newspaper, and the author of a playbook entitled *Let's Laugh About Sex.* She is also the creator and facilitator of the Humor-at-Large Workshop Series, which combines the healing aspects of humor with techniques designed to build self-confidence and promote self-esteem. Since 1993 Williams has produced the annual National Women's Comedy Conference, dubbed HotelFest, which is designed to establish a network and community of women and men interested in women's comedy, held each year in Columbus, Ohio.

A native New Yorker, Williams lived on the West Coast for many years. Currently she resides, shops, and writes on the North Coast (Ohio) while she continues to perform nationally and globally.

karen williams

Cash Flow Makes Me Come

I know that women's festivals, aka *lesbian festivals,* are supposed to be a celebration of women's culture, but why do they always have to involve camping? Camping seems to be the national sport of lesbians. But I don't understand camping. Maybe it's because I'm from New York. We don't call it *camping,* we call it *homeless!* I am not leaving my apartment to go lie outside.

I'm waiting for the ultimate festival . . . *HOTELFEST!* Roll back my sheets! Although it is kinda funny watching about eight butches trying to put up a dome tent. After about forty-eight hours, you might have some place to lie down. While they're working on putting up the tent, I become a total femme tent-site hostess, serving them drinks and snacks. Once the tent's up, I have the inside looking like a Maui condo!

There's so many things to figure out when you're a lesbian. Like how you should feel about S/M. Well, I decided to look into S/M for myself, so I went to the Ms. San Francisco Leather

Contest just to see what all the fuss is about. When I got there, everyone was walking around with their escorts on leashes, which was OK by me. But being an African-American, I have to say that the sound of the whips cracking took me someplace I didn't really want to go.

I can't quite figure out fashion either. Like I know that a man invented pantyhose. They are the world's worst contraption. When you're tall, they're a nightmare! People say to me, "Gee, Karen, you walk so demure." Not really. It's just that my crotch is down to my knees. So I decided to try the queen size. Well, that was handy. They doubled as a bra!

It's especially confusing trying to figure out who the lesbians are. After all, I was living in the San Francisco Bay Area, where I thought that every woman was a dyke. It didn't even matter if she was married to a man, I figured she had *dyke potential!* I brought that same mentality with me when I moved to the Midwest, where I quickly found out that every woman who wears a plaid shirt, jeans, and Birkenstocks is not a lesbian. They call them farmers there! What a rude awakening!

I just can't stand Birkenstocks, the official shoe of lesbians. Mostly because they're not a whole shoe, and because all of my friends insist that they're politically correct and they're safe, and that the high heels that I love to wear are not. But I say that "safe" is relative. If someone is running after me, trying to assault me, I'd rather beat them with a three-inch spike heel any day. You start beating someone with a Birkenstock and they'll think they're getting Rolfed!

Besides, I'm tired of being politically correct. Because it makes you intolerant and there are a lot of things today that people are just completely intolerant about. Like smoking. We treat smokers worse than lepers. I travel all over this country and I see people hovering together outside of office buildings, smoking, smoking, smoking, eyes darting back and forth while people walk by them, glaring at them, spitting and cursing at them, throwing money at them thinking they're homeless. It's so unfair! Did people treat us like that in the sixties? We were blowing our brains out with drugs and nobody treated us the way we treat cigarette smokers. We've gotten self-righteous.

And the most self-righteous group today are those damn vegetarians. They're so annoying because you don't get any warning when one of your friends is about to become one. One day you're sitting together at Hamburger Mary's munching on your favorite double cheeseburger, and the next time you dine together your friend is snidely commenting on your propensity for dead flesh—and feels that it's her duty to inform you that you are, in fact, eating dead flesh. I always tell 'em I prefer it that way. I hate when the flesh moves around on my plate.

It's all a setup because they haven't told you that they're vegetarians. They watch you order meat, and while you're eating it, they're forming their mental judgments. Then after you sit back exclaiming how good the meal is, they rudely and pompously inform you that they don't eat meat, that they find the practice of eating meat barbaric, that people who eat meat are disgusting, vile, smell bad, and are aggressive.

Next time this happens to you, retort that as a meat eater you are supporting our lagging economy. First of all, the beef and pork—"the other white meat"—and poultry industry of America is behind you. As for smelling bad, the deodorant, soap, perfume, douche, shampoo, and mouthwash industries are behind you. And as for being aggressive, why, the entire war machine of the planet is behind you with every bite.

I used to live in California, where nobody eats at all. My friends would call me up and say, "Let's do lunch!" So I wouldn't eat all morning, and then I'd join them for lunch. "What are you eating?" "Oh, I'll have a yogurt." "I'll have some tofu." Tofu! What is tofu? I throw my old sponges away!

You see, I can't figure this food stuff out. I don't know if it's a class thing or not, but I'm trying to get to a point where I eat steak at every meal. I want the waitperson to come up to me and say, "Ms. Williams, an appetizer?" "Oh, no thanks, I'll have a steak!" "After-dinner mint?" "Oh no, I'll have a steak!"

Then you get those people that can't eat anything. No sugar. You see, I don't know about you, but I'm not naturally that sweet; I need some sugar. No whole grains. What is holding your ass together? No preservatives. Well, that's when I really put my foot down, because I have a minimum daily requirement of preservatives. We live in the threat of a nuclear holocaust. I am not going up in a tofu poof! I want as many preservatives holding my thin ass together as possible.

I have to admit that I've tried to be more conscious about my diet. My friends convinced me to eat more organic foods and vegetables. So I went into the health food store to buy some chicken. Well, I'll admit it was bigger and plumper, but the damn thing cost me thirteen dollars—for a chicken! I took that chicken home and sat it in my living room and told it to vacuum. For thirteen dollars, I wanted it to do something else besides lie in my oven.

And, of course, I can't figure this sex stuff out. Women are still really repressed, especially lesbians. The first time I heard two lesbians talking about *who's a top, who's a bottom,* I said, "What are they talking about—PAJAMAS?" I can't figure this stuff out.

Now, I read those personal ads in the gay and lesbian newspapers and I have to tell you that the gay guys are completely way out there: "Wanted: Thick, throbbing, oozing, pulsating hunk of raw red meat NOW!" Then I look at the women's ads: "I want a woman who can read!" We've come a long way, baby!

Even in the area of safe sex, a man pulls out a condom, it's obvious what body part it's for. We're stuck with something for your teeth! What the hell is a dental dam? I've been going to the dentist for years and I've never seen a dental dam. I feel like all the dentists in America are down in their basements unpacking old boxes of dental dams *just for the lesbians!*

Now that the FDA has approved Saran Wrap for safer sex, lesbians who use Baggies by the bedside are considered really hip. Although I'm a little afraid that ten years from now a lesbian sex researcher is going to study the sex habits of lesbians and find out that we're all coughing up little bits of plastic!

The whole business of sex can be very humbling. I used to think I was a Sex Goddess until I dated a younger woman and then I found out that I was really the Goddess of Sleep! She wanted to knock boots till the break of dawn and I wanted to count my CDs and T-bills.

But a lot of old issues get resolved when you date a younger woman. Like the age-old controversy about monogamy versus nonmonogamy. I simply told her, "Goooo, fuck somebody else, stay out all night, have a great time. Goooo, I need my sleep!"

The younger lesbians today seem so bold, so out there. I went to a lesbian sex workshop and the topic was "What Turns You On!" Those young dykelings, with their butt plugs around their necks and their disposable dildos hanging out of their pockets, were talking about sexual techniques I've never even heard of. I was outraged and upset.

So I felt obligated to speak out for the over-forty crowd. I stood up to speak and the moderator said, "So, Karen, what turns you on?" And I said, "Power and cash flow! Cash flow makes me come! If you have a steady job, I'm yours for the night!" And all of the women over forty shouted and cheered and I felt proud that I'd done us justice. Because your priorities change as you get older. Mostly because it takes you longer to get to your priorities!

Like going out. I used to love to go out dancing three or four nights a week. In the seventies, it was me and Donna Summer! Now, if I want to go out on Saturday night, I have to start planning on Monday. I tell my lover that we're going out on Saturday night and we talk about it all week. On Wednesday, hump day, we decide what we're gonna wear. On Friday night we put our outfits out. Then on Saturday, about seven P.M., we look at each other and I say, yawning, "Honey, do you still want to go out?" So we watch the seven o'clock news, and then watch the eight o'clock movie . . . because the good people don't come to the club until midnight . . . so then we watch the ten o'clock news because it may have changed since seven. Then we fall asleep, and when we wake up about two A.M., we look at each other and exclaim that the good people have probably gone home. We haven't been out in four years!

Now on Saturday night, she gets the potato chips and I get the Cheez Doodles and we just sit in armchairs munching and reminiscing, because the good thing about getting older is that anything that you think that you want to do, if you just sit still long enough and think about it, you've already done it!

You don't even have to make sense anymore! You can just ramble on and on and on and people think that you're being wise. When you're young, you have to have so much passion and anger and angst and commitment in everything you utter. But when you get older, you can just say anything and people assume that there's some deep meaning in it. Although I must admit that I have a few friends that try to use that same technique to impress me, only they do it using big words used improperly. Like they say, "Karen, I've made a New Year's *revolution.*" Or, "I feel really *disorientated* today" (is "disorientated" a word?). Or I showed a friend of mine an apartment and she said, "Excuse me, are the blinds *velour*?" Now, I know she meant *Levolor,* but when she left I went over to touch them just to make sure they weren't fuzzy!

People take themselves so seriously. Like New Yorkers. They're really proud of their ability to make it in a virtual war zone. In New York, LIFE IS A WAR! And then I moved to California, where LIFE IS A BEACH! Now I live in the Midwest, where LIFE IS A BREWSKI! Such different mentalities about things.

Like when I try to cash a check in the Midwest. In California anything with zeros on it is considered currency. You can make out a check on a napkin and a store clerk will accept it and cash it. But I tried to cash a check in Ohio and the clerk wanted to see my two living parents as proof of my identity. Actually, she asked me for my Ohio driver's license, which I didn't have yet because I wasn't sure if I was staying in Ohio, so I showed her my passport instead. I'm sure it was the first time this clerk had ever seen a black woman with a passport. So she asked me where was I from. It took everything I had not to say *Kenya!* I wanted to dance around like Kunta Kinte: "Oombali, Ommbali, Oomwaillee!" But instead I said, "California!" And

she said, "You need a passport to come from California to
Ohio!" I ran out of the store!

I was scared for that clerk, but that's only because I'm
codependent. But then all moms are codependent. But it's not
our fault. We're only human and we breed codependency.

I've often wondered why we can't be like other lowly creatures, who have the good sense to lay an egg outside of themselves and let that little creature peck its own butt out of its own
shell right from the beginning. Rabbits have little bunnies and
they're hopping away from the mama in a matter of minutes.
Horses have little ponies and they're galloping away in no time
at all. And birds are real straightforward. They push the little
ones out of the nest and say, "Fly!"

We give birth to something that can't hold up its own head
and doesn't leave the nest for eighteen years. And we feel guilty
when they leave. Now, if that's not codependent, I don't know
what is!

I find it hard to relate to my own kids. I was a real nerd, a
bookworm. I carried twelve books home from school every
day. I was the only kid on line on Friday afternoons waiting for
the bookmobile. I find it hard to relate to people sitting around
watching television. It seems like a gross waste of time.

But what really pisses me off are those stupid soap operas.
Why, those aren't real people at all! First thing in the morning,
those women are perfectly coiffed and made up. Now, I don't
know about you, but when I wake up in the morning, I have a

radical case of bedhead. I have hair sculptures. Those women have no crust in the eyes or dried drool on their lips, and they're kissing and making love first thing in the morning. They never wake up and have to go pee! The only reason I wake up in the morning at all is biological. Romance is not on my mind.

I think this romance stuff is overrated anyway. Who were we supposed to learn it from . . . our parents! We grow up with so many mixed messages that we get used to them.

Like the last relationship I was in, the woman was reading *Journey of a Solitude* and I was reading *Permanent Partners,* so it doesn't surprise me that things didn't work out.

My mom was a mixed-message queen. She used to tuck me in at night and say, "I love you, I love you, I love you so well, / If I had a peanut, I'd give you the shell." Well, needless to say, I was a chronic insomniac as a child as I stayed awake all night trying to figure out, "What, I wasn't good enough to get the whole peanut!"

Fortunately, I've learned to pray, so let's close with the Ambiguity Prayer. Please repeat after me: "Goddess (because we know it's a woman), grant me the serenity to accept the things I cannot change, the courage to change the things I can, and the wisdom to know when to kick butt when things don't go my way . . ."

acknowledgments

I would like to express my gratitude to the many people who helped make *Out, Loud, & Laughing* possible. My publisher, Martha Levin, and Executive Editor Charlie Conrad were invaluable resources from the start. Tom Viola and Zack Manna of Broadway Cares/Equity Fights AIDS were always generous in their promotional efforts for this project. Art Director Mario Pulice produced a cover as *fabulous* as himself. Bob Daniels was everything an editor and fifteen comics could want in a copy editor: patient, scrupulous, and kind. All of the contributors and their agents were overwhelmingly supportive in their response to the project, and I would especially like to thank those who early on helped this project grow: Jaffe Cohen, Frank DeCaro, Brian Freeman, Mark Kelley, Frank Maya, and Irene Pinn.

Finally, for their support and encouragement, I would like to thank Hamilton Cain, Delia Kurland, Arabella Meyer, Jay Yokley, and Michael Zam, who never failed to laugh, even when the jokes weren't mine.

Grateful acknowledgment is made to the following for permission to print their copyrighted material.

Clinton: "Could Lesbians Return?" copyright © 1995 by Kate Clinton. Printed by permission of the author.

Cohen: "My Life as a Heterosexual" first appeared in *New York Native*. Copyright © 1987 by Jaffe Cohen. Reprinted by permission of the author.

Cytron and Malinowitz: Excerpts from *A Dyke Grows in Brooklyn* and *Take My Domestic Partner—Please!* copyright © 1995 by Sara Cytron and Harriet Malinowitz. Printed by permission of the authors.

DeCaro: "So What Constitutes a Homosexual Act?" first appeared in *New York Newsday* (7/27/93). Copyright © 1993 by Frank DeCaro. Reprinted by permission of the author. "You Are What You Serve" first appeared in *New York Newsday* (1/18/94). Copyright © 1994 by Frank DeCaro. Reprinted by permission of the author. "1997's Biggest Controversy: *Haute* Crime" first appeared in *New York Newsday* (2/9/93). Copyright © 1993 by Frank DeCaro. Reprinted by permission of the author.

DeLaria: "Ms. DeLaria's Dating Tips for Dykes" copyright © 1995 by Lea DeLaria. Printed by permission of the author.

Foster: "Nelson Volunteers" copyright © 1995 by Emmett Foster. Printed by permission of the author.

Gomez: Excerpt from *Marga Gomez Is Pretty, Witty & Gay* copyright © 1995 by Marga Gomez. Printed by permission of the author.

Maya: Excerpt from *Paying for the Pool* copyright © 1995 by Frank Maya. Printed by permission of the author.

Moore: "AIDS—God, I Hope I Never Get That Again" copyright © 1995 by Steve Moore. Printed by permission of the author.

Planet Q: "*Lesbian Jeopardy!*" copyright © 1995 by Ann Stengel. Printed by permission of the author. "Life with Leviticus" copyright © 1995 by Chrisanne Eastwood. Printed by permission of the author. "Lesbian Bed Death" copyright © 1995 by Chrisanne Eastwood. Printed by permission of the author.

Pomo Afro Homos: "QVC/Queer Value Channel" and "Towards a Black Queer Rhythm Nation" copyright © 1995 by Pomo Afro Homos. Printed by permission of the authors.

Sedaris: "*Glen's Homophobia Newsletter, Vol. 3, No. 2*" from *Barrel Fever* by David Sedaris. Copyright © 1994 by David Sedaris. Reprinted by permission of Little, Brown and Company.

about the editor

Charles Flowers is an Associate Editor at Anchor Books. He lives in New York City. According to sources, he's a real hoot.

Broadway Cares/ Equity Fights AIDS

Since October 1987, Broadway Cares/Equity Fights AIDS (BC/EFA) has raised and distributed millions of dollars in the fight against AIDS. These funds have been disbursed in response to thousands of requests for personal financial assistance from PWAs (People with AIDS) in the entertainment industry nationwide and as grants to hundreds of AIDS service organizations from coast to coast. BC/EFA is committed to doing whatever it takes for as long as it takes to provide comfort for and assistance to those living with HIV and AIDS, and continues to do all within its power to promote a rational response across America to this epidemic that affects us all. Anchor Books is proud to assist in this endeavor by donating all net royalties from the sale of this book to BC/EFA.

Anchor Books